Echo Chamber

The Second 56-weeks of POTUS 45

Echo Chamber
The Second 56-weeks of POTUS 45

Books may be ordered through booksellers or by contacting:
www.createspace.com/#######
www.Amazon.com

———————

CreateSpace Title ID: #######
Jacked Design & Illustrations © Guebres Studios

ISBN-13: 9781090642882(sc)
ISBN-10: ######### (ebk)

Printed in the United States of America
CreateSpace date: 00/00/2018

It all begins with that which has gone before; It ends on something new that was known before. Common truth in life, bought once, it will be bought twice. Just allow a time between each sale. The hard reality of existence relies on the simple truth – everything is the same, they just change the name.
~ a High School science realization, c.1958

"What we do see depends mainly on what we look for. In the same field the farmer will notice the crop, the geologists the fossils, botanists the flowers, artists the coloring, sportsmen the cover for the game. Though we may all look at the same things, it does not all follow that we should see them."
~ John Lubbock

"The fault-finder will find faults even in paradise. ... The setting sun is reflected from the windows of the alms-house as brightly as from the rich man's abode; the snow melts before its door as early in the spring. ..."
~ Henry David Thoreau, Walden, 1854

"What do you do with the mad that you feel
"When you feel so mad you could bite?
"When the whole wide world seems oh, so wrong...
"And nothing you do seems very right?
"It's great to be able to stop
"When you've planned a thing that's wrong,
"And be able to do something else instead..."
~ Fred M. Rogers, 1968

"Only those who will risk going too far can possibly find out how far one can go."
~ T.S. Eliot

You will never go as far as you dream, nor fall as far as you fear. The world is really that horrible, but it is also perfect and beautiful. Open your eyes and view reality – or close them and let it kick you in the ass...

CHAPTERS

CHAPTER ONE – *Believing is Seeing.*
You see what you believe you should see.

Most people are familiar with Hans Christian Anderson and his stories – the creation of "Perception Bias" is the basis of THE EMPEROR'S NEW CLOTHES, where people deny the evidence of their own eyes because they were told their intelligence would be judged based on their seeing what they were told they should see.

The term "Echo Chamber' has been adopted as a metaphor describing a human tendency to either subconsciously select or consciously decide to be exposed to information which reinforces pre-existing beliefs or, as with the Emperor's New Clothes, accepts what is commonly accepted, for fear of being deemed ignorant.

But we know this, and embrace it in the same way people have been embracing it throughout human history.

How does Trump want to be seen, and how would Russia or some Disruptive Actor wish him to be seen?

How does America want to be seen?

We need only follow the news and social media to see and understand how Americans wish the world to view them.

Americans have declared there is something wrong with the Constitution, that the idea of an Electoral College having the final say over the interpretation of the popular vote is wrong. Clearly, if Americans argue their voting system was wrong in 2016, it must also have been wrong for the previous 228-years.

Americans have questioned the Intelligence Quotient [IQ] of their duly elected President. But, since his methods resulted in a win, how dim-witted must the loser have been? And, if he is a habitual liar – one who apparently lied better than his dim-witted opponent – stupid must their respective supporters be?

In the Emperor's New Clothes, the scam artists presented an invisible fabric which could only the highly intelligent could see and appreciate. Americans are declaring their Party Leaders to be no better than those tailors – but, while we can ask what we were supposed to see, what we discover is that we are supposed to see what we do NOT want, with no inkling of what we really want.

When the World looks at America, it sees a nation opposed. A nation being opposed by its own people, who are challenging the design of their own Constitution.

The voters in 20-percent of the states were opposed to Donald, while the remaining 80-percent opposed Hillary. If we look at the facts, electorally, the majority of the voters are in the minority of states, and that basic fact represents the very reality the Founding Fathers had taken into account when the established a Representative House, and a State representing Senate.

The Founding Fathers wanted to ensure all the States had an equal voice in government. This included the design of the Electoral College and the separate judiciary represented by the Supreme Court.

In the Trump Era, Facts are a problem. Maya Angelou said it: *"There's a world of difference between truth and facts. Facts can obscure the truth."*

What are the facts? A native New Yorker, a businessman who is best known from his 'Reality TV' presentation and habit of putting his name on everything, challenges Reagan Conservatives for control of the Republican Party.

Emerging from the State that gave us a Depression ending New Deal creating, Nazi defeating, polio debilitated POTUS of a newly emerging liberal Democratic Party, Trump proved the fallacy of Reaganomics – a program based on crushing debt to be escaped by the fraud of economy-crushing inflation which would fraudulently erase the debt through an apparent Ponzi Scheme of monetization – and then Trump predicates his campaign on the full acceptance and funding of Reagan opposed border security.

Where Franklin Delano Roosevelt was born in the wealthy upstate community of Hyde Park, in Dutchess County, New York, Donald John Trump came from the working class Queens County borough of New York City.

And, while FDR was descended from the original Dutch settlers who predated the arrival of Mayflower settlers, DJT was of the second generation born to an anti-war German immigrant who made his money by being conservative and playing it safe – providing lodging to those seeking wealth in the Klondike Gold Rush, rather than venturing into the wilds and panning for gold himself. Yet, despite their obvious historic differences, in terms of kinship, they are sixteenth cousins, and in terms of ideologies they both wanted a prosperous nation – so it should be no surprise that the infamous 'America First' policy for which Trump has been attacked was rooted in the 1932 speech where his cousin declared, *"In this respect **I am for America first.**"* This is the same cousin who was, and will remain, the only President elected four times.

We tend to forget that the Great Depression was brought to us by Republican Herbert Clark Hoover; that Prohibition and the criminal activity and murders associated with it were given us by Republican Evangelicals seeking control over the lives of average workers – much that their 'pro-life' descendants are today when they preach against abortion while asserting moral acceptability in allowing both mother and fetus to die when an abortion would save the mother and allow her to have the viable child she desires.

Democrats ignore or accept far Right-wing Republicans spending billions to murder people in foreign lands, but close the government over an amount approximating one-one-thousandth of America's fiscal Budget. They ignore the fact that the funds are to improve upon a structure the lead opponent of the expenditure, their Senate Leader, Chuck Schumer, had fought for and achieved with the 2006 Secure Fence Act. They now make wild claims that Fences do not control illegal entry into the nation, and yet, completion of the section along the California border was followed by a decline in illegal or undocumented migrants from Mexico.

There is a bit of contextual history passage needed to when talking of the 2006 Secure Fence Act. The border Fence was pure Democrat when, in 1980, Ronald Reagan chastised Bush: *"Rather than making them, of talking about putting up a fence, why don't we work out some recognition of our mutual problems, make it possible for them to come here legally with a work permit, and then, while they're working and earning here, they pay taxes here."*

So either Reagan was opposed to a Democratic Fence or a Bush Fence; clearly, he was in favor of an open border based on legal entry and documentation that allowed tax collection. With a Fence/Wall and lawful border crossing processing, Mexicans or Mexico would be paying for structures allowing legal entry.

But in 2006, it came in the context of 9/11 and George W Bush declared: *"This bill will help protect the American people. This bill will make our borders more secure. It is an important step toward immigration reform."*

So we hear of the Reagan Immigration Reform melded into Democratic Border Security in the context of a stunning terrorist attack on American landmark structures – accompanied by the murder of a diverse group of nearly 2,974 citizens by 19 terrorists who committed suicide. Of course, in the aftermath, more died.

On 13 September 2006, Peter Thomas King introduced the legislation – King had been elected, as a Nassau County, New York Republican Congressman, concurrent with Bill Clinton's victory, and Clinton had carried Nassau County by a 15% margin over GHW Bush. King proved himself to be a staunch opponent of Ted Cruz and had considered running for the Presidency in 2016 – as with New York Democrats, King is also an advocate of strong gun control and improving Healthcare coverage beyond the levels offered under Obamacare, a fact which aligns him with both Bernie Sanders and Donald Trump.

In 2006, the estimated 25-year cost of the fence, including all maintenance, was estimated to be $50 billion – approximately $2 Billion annually, or half of the amount now needed by Trump to compensate for the lack of funding under previous Conservative or Reagan Republican Controlled Congresses.

Reagan Democrats routinely referenced the decline sharp decline in apprehensions associated with illegal crossings. If we look at the 2000-2018 monthly March figures published by THE WIRE on under the title "The Stats on Border Apprehensions," on 6 April 2018, we see that all the numbers prior to 2008, when the first phase of the Fence was completed, were higher than those in subsequent years.

Prior to the legislation, in March 2006, there were 160,000 arrests. After the first 613 miles of the Fence had come into use, the numbers dropped to about 65,000 – that is a statistical known reduction of about 60% and infers the Fence was working. And if we look at the period associated with Trump's tough rhetoric of 2015/16 initiated a further drop to about 30,000, which continued until the Reagan Democrats began their struggle for reversal of the Fence policy – in March 2017, arrests had fallen to 10,000 or less than 6.25% of where they were prior to the Fence legislation, and less than 4.25% of the peak 220,000 presented by THE WIRE fact checking article.

So, as we see Reagan Republicans exhibit Climate Change

denial, we see their Reagan Democrat counterparts exhibit a much stronger Fence Effectiveness denial – where the effectiveness is clearly shown in all the available hard numbers.

A second chart in the 6 April article showed the number of apprehensions from 1960 to 2017 and revealed a steady growth that peaked during the Reagan Administration Amnesty of 1886 – 1.6 million apprehensions. This number was only exceeded with the 2000 election of GW Bush, then falling with the 2001 events of 9/11 and dropping for the next two years, while migrants at the Southern Border determined if they wished to live in a nation that was a terrorist target – then, with Bush's Middle Eastern war, the numbers rebound sharply to increase by over 30% from their low.

Once again, with only 649 miles of fencing completed along the 2,000-mile border, the number of apprehensions plummeted from their Bush high of about 1.65 million to about 325 thousand in 2011 when Obama and Schumer were trash-talking illegals and threatening to send their kids back across the border without any regard for what happened to them afterward.

Thus, tough Trump-style talk, in combination with only a partially competed Fence, created an 80% drop in illegal border crossing apprehensions. Naturally, this then affected the statistics so we would hear the distraction of subsequent undocumented aliens being comprised of those who overstay their legal visa. The fact that a fence has no relevance to the actions of someone who legally entered the nation – as the 9/11 Terrorists did – seems to be beyond the limited intelligence of the target demographic for such arguments.

Nor do those making the assertive comparison note that they are counting those who are "between documents" – foreign-born spouses shifting from the 90 day fiancee visa to the post-marriage permanent status, and others seeking to extend, amend or alter, their legal status, who are undocumented due to resource and personnel shortages within Immigration and Naturalization Services.

The statistical reality is that the Fence (or Wall) works, and because it works so well, the statistics have revealed the flaws in the legal entry side of the undocumented immigrant issue. The case against Reagan's 1980 attacks on Fence construction, clearly been proven by the objective evidence, is no better than his ideas, once called "Voodoo Economics" but now known as Reaganomics.

Having disproved Reaganomics, Trump is associated with promoting an iconic structure with Reagan opposed and is now opposed by the emerging Reagan Democrats who seem opposed to everything Reagan opposed – as was shown in their opposition to the Socialist-Progressive-Liberal policies put forward by Bernie Sanders.

If we look at the actions – or, as it was commanded, *"know them by their deeds"* – Americans are opposed to States having an equal voice. If they were honest about the Electoral College, then citizens oppose an Electoral College determining Trump's victory would also oppose the State representation in the Senate, where the population size is ignored and the smallest states gain the largest population count voice.

Think about the calls which began with announcement of the 2016 elections results – immediate impeachment of Trump, and, if successful for the first time in history, replace him with a staunch Right-wing Theocratic Evangelical-style adulterer whose view of human rights is that they have none unless it is subservient to his misrepresentation of scripture and Ponzi scheme deficit approach to economics.

Would changing things actually change things?

Clearly, Reagan Republicans were hidden among emerging Democratic leaders, and they are seeking to assume power, while Trump seems to be promoting an FDR Democrat approach to the nation's future. Yet, Trump ran as a Republican – which should make the few Christians who know the Bible laugh: after all, Jesus was attacked for consorting with 'low life-types', and Trump set the goal of Draining the Swamp, which means you must go to the swamp you wish to drain – he might not have realized the real swamp was the hidden denizens who are now emerging as Reagan Democrats like Chuck Schumer and, possibly, Nancy Pelosi.

Would civility toward others replace mobs who are in the opposition? Would it even make clear what those who oppose are actually opposed to?

During the Bret Kavanaugh SCOTUS nomination hearings, the World witnessed attacks based on unsubstantiated allegations of improper teenage behavior four decades earlier. The Statues of individuals from the Civil War era were being attacked by people who ignored the children starving in Yemen today, and ignoring all that was happening to threaten their future tomorrow?

Then, on 28 November, with the Democrats having won the House, a striking majority of senators voted to move forward a bill ending three years of Obama era support for a Saudi-led coalition fighting in Yemen. This marked a shift from the murder of Saudi journalist Jamal Khashoggi to a proper focus on condemnation of a policy linked to hundreds of alleged war crimes and deaths of tens of thousands of innocents.

Just seven days before the Midterm Election, the Nation witnessed, and ignored, Senate Majority Leader Mitch McConnell floated an idea of slashing Social Security and Medicaid benefits at a time when the Baby-Boomers were turning seventy and shifting to Social Security at the rate of 10,000 per day.

He was threatening the income of over 15-percent of the American population. In 2016, there were roughly 323.4 million Americans; of those, 231.5 million were eligible to vote; of those, 57.5-percent actually voted. That means Senator McConnell was threatening income security or healthcare for about 48.5 million voters – 22-percent of the total, and possibly a third of those who actually took the time to vote.

If we take into account those on 'safety-net' programs, we have more voters than voted in the 2016 election – yet McConnell has no trouble attacking their prospects for survival. How stupid are the American people – given that McConnell clearly believed, and was saying, they are self-destructive idiots?

The November 2018 election results shed some light on the collective IQ. In that context, the vote reflected the idea expressed by feminist essayist Anais Nin: *"We don't see things as they are, we see them as we are."* Because of that, people vote based on the fantasy politicians are able to sell. They also tend to reject those more obvious fantasies – Trump has the ability to push fantasy to the point of disbelief; as a result, the Democrats won control of the House, and with it, control of the House committees which are in the best position to stop the Right-wing's "Most Harm to the Most People" agenda.

As the results rolled in, Trump tweeted his reaction: *"In all fairness, Nancy Pelosi deserves to be chosen Speaker of the House by the Democrats. If they give her a hard time, perhaps we will add some Republican votes. She has earned this great honor!"*

As Speaker, Pelosi would need to make serious choices for the nation. If she gets mired down in childish political games, it could crash the economy.

For several decades, American has been experiencing what is called a *"productivity-pay gap"* which amounts to the onset of de facto economic slavery which threatens to create class warfare of a type that often leads to revolution.

Increases in pay have almost kept pace with the artificially calculated rate of inflation – a rate which ignores reality and can be used to suppress adjustments to inflation-adjusted income like Social Security.

Now, in 2018, with a booming Stock Market that is seen as evidence of increased national wealth, accompanied by record low levels of unemployment associated with the demographic shift of aging Baby-Boomers moving into retirement with NPG (Negative Population Growth) reducing the number of replacement workers, the nation should be seeing solid pay increases. But it isn't, and this has many economists wondering why the higher demand for workers has failed to translate into larger pay increases.

The economic disconnect has been termed a *'Wage Puzzle'* which has wage growth at two-thirds the rate it should be – even taking into consideration it's a midterm election year, but might be fully consistent with the fact that the President has been under fire and there was the threat of continued Right-wing Republican control being offset by the possibility that some radical Left-wing victory will result in what economists know would be an economy-destroying impeachment proceeding.

The *'Wage Puzzle'* might find an answer in 26 November announcement by General Motors that it will be laying-off 14,000 workers in Canada and the United States, with plans for additional plant closing after 2019. This follows an industry-wide drop in new car sales – something which will continue as the Baby-Boom generation ages/dies. GM is moving into electric vehicles and the cost savings will fund the new, climate-protecting, technology.

Every nation has its divides. Traditionally, they have been in the areas of economics, religion, and government or the politics of leadership. America has proven it is the same as every other nation. When Americans seek meaning, they look at family, their careers or employment, and any friendships they can rely upon. When they convinced they should attack their leaders – without just cause – they forget what gives meaning to life.

In an orderly society, health is a major factor. People who are healthy will tolerate a great deal; in North Korean {DPRK} the citizens enjoy the Universal Health Care denied American citizens, and so they accept many things deemed intolerable in America.

The DPRK has food shortages, which it can blame on those outside its borders. Until Trump, America represented a major cause of hardships which served to justify their development of nuclear capability – America attacks Asian nations; it even attacks its own people.

Trump, comes from a family whose patriarch escaped to America, rather than be a conscripted German mercenary; his line is successful, and therefore hated for the same reason's the Jews have been hated.

Trump has been called low IQ; in 1900, Jewish immigrants were deemed the dumbest of people, by 1912, their children were flooding the halls of Harvard in such numbers that they were being turned away and the famed University being denounced for antisemitism in the same way it was attacked for discrimination in 2018. Albert Einstein once said, *"The true sign of intelligence is not knowledge but imagination."*

Trump imagines a nation with the kind of growth Obama began and he managed to sustain and expand upon. Wages are going up, but it will take Democratic legislation to raise the Federal Minimum Wage and also raise the cap on Social Security FICA contributions so that the benefits can be raised and retirees need not see those benefits supplemented by public assistance.

It seems the math is over the heads of those who denounce ever increasing Public Assistance claims caused by 10,000 retirees per day discovering they paid in for 40-years only to be ripped-off and denied a dignified retirement they were promised. One reality is that there is now an over-reliance on Social Security which means the current level of underfunding promoted by the Republican Party (without Democratic objection)creates a long-term danger. Since 1985, the second term of Reagan's Voodoo Economics era, the Social Security Board of Trustees' annual report has warned that the program wouldn't generate enough long-term revenue to cover expenditures through 2060.

With the combined death of the Baby-boomers, which will happen before 2050, and Negative Population Growth which is going to cause a Baby-Bust, this infers serious economic dangers for the Millennials retiring between 2050 and 2060 – which will be compounded by Climate Change effects.

In simpler terms, the program is going to spend way more money by issuing benefits to eligible recipients than it's going to collect from its payroll tax on earned income, the taxation of benefits, and interest income on its nearly $2.9 trillion in asset reserves.

During the American revolution, German mercenaries fought for the British; since the 2nd World War, the de facto mercenaries have been Americans "protecting" regimes opposed by their own people. This all came to an end with the breakup of the Soviet Union and end of the Cold War, which led to Russian bankruptcy in 1998. Russia emerged as a capitalist nation with a solid class of billionaires, while America has continued to fund NATO, which is now only an economic stimulus for Germany and the economy of the European Union.

A Trump Twitter post dated 10:11 27 January 2019, stated: *"Jens Stoltenberg, NATO Secretary General, just stated that because of me NATO has been able to raise far more money than ever before from its members after many years of decline. It's called burden sharing. Also, more united. Dems & Fake News like to portray the opposite!"* It would appear Trump's approach worked, and NATO members were beginning to carry their fair part of the post-Cold War load. If that proved to be the case over the ensuing years, America, with its troops NOT stationed there, should be in a far better position to defend the European Union.

About four weeks before the 2018 Midterm election, former Vice-President Joe Biden repeated the warning he gave prior to the 23 June 2016 BREXIT vote. Speaking at Chatham House, the British Royal Institute of International Affairs, Biden said, *"There is a special relationship, we have been locked cheek and jowl on almost every important issue that exists, and so without England being totally integrated in the EU to the extent that it is distanced from that diminishes our ability to have influence on events on the continent."*

Biden also pointed out that there were forces at work that were *"increasingly meddling in free societies and exploiting the openness of our systems to sow chaos and influence political outcomes by using the tools available to them, which include information warfare and propaganda, economic coercion, corruption, energy manipulation and even, as we have seen here in Great Britain, assassinations."*

Recognizing the commercial aspect of the problem, Trump had, instinctively, recognized BREXIT mandated the Trade-based related policies required adjustments – if the EU disintegrated, it would trigger economic problems like those emerging in Greece, Turkey, Italy, and even Germany. These are problems that could culminate in an economic meltdown around the year 2027.

By voting for BREXIT, Britain voted to reduced American influence in the European Union, but also could force the various nations to reassess their laws. We know the EU nations were not fully compliant with the Paris Climate Accords, and in the case of their agricultural policy their farm subsidy system actually works against the Accords by subsidizing deforestation of land that is unsuited for agriculture, but for which subsidies are paid when it is reduced to an "agricultural condition." Phrased another way, the EU is paying corporations purchase small farms, consolidate and then destroy natural systems which remove atmospheric CO_2 and convert the climate-damaging gases to life-sustaining oxygen.

When Biden spoke of those who *"sow chaos and influence political outcomes,"* he was speaking of the use of propaganda or common sales techniques, but, it turned out, he was also speaking of Schumer's Reagan Democrats.

Propaganda and sales function in the same way: get people nodding yes, then hear your pitch so they respond in the affirmative to each new suggestion, escalate each suggestion toward your ultimate goal -- closing the deal, making the "sale", or controlling their thinking. If you can implant an idea that furthers your objective, the goal being to establish a level where people are predisposed to acceptance of the new variation on the theme; twisting facts to conform to that theme or idea becomes easy.

"Crooked Hillary" and "Trump the liar" are the current themes whose objective is the same -- undermine Global trust in the American government by having the citizens assert their government is untrustworthy, and proving this idea by having the citizens themselves challenge and object to their own Constitution or basic principles of law and fair play. Assigning guilt without hard factual evidence, and challenging the rationale behind the electoral college, have proved very effective; so much so that North Korea date not enter an agreement with an America where street mobs are actively supporting lawlessness.

The day before Biden's speech, former First Lady and 2016 Presidential Candidate Hillary Clinton was interviewed at Oxford College in Oxford, England, where she was asked about the newly coined pejorative term "*swiftboating*," derived from the attacks on Senator John Kerry in 2004, with the technique later used against Mitt Romney in 2012. It is "political chicanery" which relies upon a "*baseless smear against somebody's personal character.*"

The "*swiftboating*" question was based on the rumor that Bill Clinton – who, in 1969, attended University College, Oxford on a Rhodes Scholarship – had been expelled for raping Eileen Wellstone, a 19-year-old English woman, who had claimed Clinton had sexually assaulted her after she met him at a pub near Oxford. Apparently, the matter had been investigated, and Clinton had admitted having consensual sex, and, her family declined pursuit of the matter.

Given the "Oral in the Oval" basis for impeachment charges against Clinton, it is interesting that the retired State Department employee who allegedly investigated the matter would state in an interview, "*There was no doubt in my mind that this young woman had suffered severe emotional trauma. But we were under tremendous pressure to avoid the embarrassment of having a Rhodes Scholar charged with rape. I filed a report with my superiors and that was the last I heard of it.*"

Just two days before the Hillary interview, the Senate had confirmed the Supreme Court appointment of Brett Kavanaugh, who was accused of indulging in sexual misconduct 35-years ago, when he was a teenager. In both cases, it was believed the "*young woman had suffered severe emotional trauma.*" Apart from Bill Clinton having been a 23-year old adult, actual intercourse having occurred, and the pattern of continued sexual "misconduct' which extended into his White House years, we could view some parallel between Clinton and Kavanaugh – one where the POTUS is given a free pass while the unsubstantiated claims against the teenager have led to him being vilified.

Hillary, who obviously condoned her husband's behavior, used the opportunity to assert *"you cannot be civil with a political party that wants to destroy what you stand for or what you care about. That's why I believe, if we are fortunate enough to win back the House and/or the Senate, that when civility can start again. But, until then, the only thing that the Republicans seem to recognize and respect is strength."*

Hillary then pointed to the attacks on Ford, generalizing it to all women, and then talked of *"the falsehoods and lies, which, unfortunately, people believe because Republicans have put a lot of time, money and effort into promoting them. So, when you are dealing with an ideological party which is driven by the lust for power, that is funded by corporate interests that want a government that does its bidding, you can be civil, but you can't overcome what they intend to do unless you win elections."*

Note she says, you cannot be civil unless you are *"fortunate enough to win back the House and/or Senate"*. It's a matter of luck and not work, and certainly does not require a message that is coherent and meaningful to the voters in terms that reflect any sound policies which those voters can understand as beneficial.

Why does Trump win? Is it that he knows his base or target demographic well enough to be able to, with a straight face, say,*"I Could Stand In the Middle Of Fifth Avenue And Shoot Somebody And I Wouldn't Lose Any Voters"* – which he did on 23 January 2016 – while, on 9 September 2016, Hillary, supposedly an experienced politician, called that same demographic *"a Basket of deplorables"*?

Here, in book six of the TRUMP CARD series, we look at the turning point in the American experiment, America's day six before the day of rest, the day in which man and serpent speak. Shall we bite the Apple, acquire wisdom and the pain that comes with it, or remain merely obedient animals – pets to some unseen omnipotent master?

The book which gave rise to this series, Jonathon's Potus Cousins, revealed an American reality based on a subliminal need for voters to elect presidents who were kinsman. Subsequent analysis revealed that all the Presidents were descendants of one man – William the Conqueror.

This echoes the structure of the traditional Biblical Levite ruling class where kinship strength from the Tribal to Federal level determined the strength of the nation. In the Bible, when this kinship broke down, the nation died; Biblically, 57-cycles has a significance which can be marked with Barack Obama marking the fifty-seventh POTUS cycle.

George Washington and Barack Obama are tenth cousins and connect the beginning and end of the 228-year cycle. Obama was also the last POTUS before the solar system moved into the "Age of Aquarius" – when the zodiac moved into a different house to mark the end of the Aztec/Inca Calendar and dawn of a new age – and the first "New Age" POTUS is Donald John Trump; so it is natural that we see a conflict between the Old and New Ages.

Obama was also significant because, as a mulatto, his line carried us to the origin place of African slaves whose existence in America had them a designation, fractional people. Washington marked the result of a Revolution so it seems fitting if we are to enter a new age in history, that the old age, one built on slavery, should end with a Commander-in-Chief who is a fractional African and symbolically end the race revolution which began around the time of his birth.

Of course, one of the pieces of the Obama ancestral history that few are aware of is, while both Michelle and Barack are direct descendants of the nation's founding families, Barack mother's line was also born of the first African slaves. Symbolically, Obama represents the fabric of America as defined by its first 228-years, a point in time marked by his administration.

The World witnessed the Great Recession, roughly 57-years after the Great Depression, which was itself roughly 57-years after the constitutional change that ended slavery, provided another "mystical coincidence" for the annals of history which are witness to demographic and climate-related turning points. Historically, the nation's internal events relate to major changes of significance being determined around the world.

Does Trump and his Wall have significance? Or BREXIT, and the related FREXIT which emerged in France at the same time as its British counterpart. What significance is found in the violence in or emergence of ancient historic nations seemingly struggling to reclaim their ancient roles of importance – Israel, China, Iran, and even the land defining northern India?

On 6 March 1891, Teddy Roosevelt said: "*If the minority is as powerful as the majority there is no use of having political contests at all, for there is no use in having a majority.*" Was he, in some obscure manner, denouncing the Electoral College?

Nine years earlier, President Chester A. Arthur had signed The Chinese Exclusion Act into law; between 1900 & 1908, more than 60,000 Chinese entered via Mexico – and Teddy Roosevelt had been POTUS for seven of those years. In January 1904, an editorial in the *El Paso Herald-Post* stated that, were the Chinese migration through Mexico to continue, "*it will be necessary to run a barbed wire fence along our side of the Rio Grande.*"

The Rio Grande is something of a natural barrier extending 1254 miles – one whose crossing became known as "Wetbacks." As with many things, the first fence erected along the border was built in 1909 – not to stop people, but rather to stop trans-border movement of cattle – and was constructed by the U.S. Bureau of Animal Industry, which existed between May 1884 and February 1942, when the Agricultural Research Administration assumed control, only to be abolished in November 1953.

After 1910, it was common for border towns to erect fences – fast forward to 1993 and President Bill Clinton constructed a 14-mile barrier between San Diego and Tijuana, which was intended to address a drug smuggling problem; three years later, Clinton would sign legislation granting the Attorney General the de facto power to build walls; a decade after that, Bush-43 would add 165-miles of wall that Obama would proudly declare complete.

Fences or barriers are a part of Border Control history and serve many purposes. It is a serious mistake to create a narrowly focused objection intended to undermine the broader purposes.

If the Chinese, with their distinctive Asian appearance and accent, could cross the border simply by learning a few words of Spanish – which is exactly how they circumvented the Chinese Exclusion Act to gained entry via the Mexican border – what could a modern terrorist do to gain the same entry?

In 2009, Chuck Schumer proclaimed:

"*The first of these seven principles is that illegal immigration is wrong, plain and simple. When we use phrases like 'undocumented workers,' we convey a message to the American people that their government is not serious about combating illegal immigration, which the American people overwhelmingly oppose.*

"People who enter the United States without our permission are illegal aliens, and illegal aliens should not be treated the same as people who entered the United States legally. Any immigration solution must recognize that we must do as much as we can to gain operational control of our borders as soon as possible."

Does removal of the Fence enhance *"operational control of our borders"*? Or does it enhance the ability of illegals to enter the country – possibly seeking a better life, and possibly seeking to engage in criminal activities where they are more profitable than at home?

In opposing himself, so that he can spite Trump, Schumer clearly demonstrated he doesn't care for America. If he did, his attention would be focused on providing Universal Medicare, and the providing of an above poverty minimum wage which would immediately remove millions of hard-working people from public assistance. A reality that would easily save the nation, in monthly benefits, far more than Trump needed to repair, restore, and also improve, the 650-miles or so of Border Security Fence Schumer argued for in 2006 and throughout the Obama Administration.

When Trump took office, Schumer and Pelosi did join with Bernie Sanders' proposal for $15 an hour minimum wage hike – something Sanders sought in 2012, and Schumer ignored.

It seems funny that Schumer, who voted for the Fence and the required upgrades, would allow, even force, a government shutdown over $5.7Billion, while he refuses to fight to save more than that, each and every month, with a Minimum Wage increase, thus removing all minimum wage workers from SNAP and other supplemental support programs.

Nancy Pelosi has assumed the same 1980 position Ronald Reagan held and voted against the Fence Act, so her position to all border security is consistent. Should the Trump nonsense about terrorists crossing prove prophetic, Pelosi would then be the agent who facilitated their actions.

In 2016, 701,000 workers were earning exactly the $7.25 per hour federal minimum wage – a total of 2.2 million workers earned at or below the federal minimum. All of them qualified for public assistance. And, with the Shutdown based on Schumer's refusal to allow Trump one 1000th of the Federal Budget for the Fence Schumer argued was necessary, Schumer was struggling to increase those numbers – so Trump's economy would look bad.

As a Senator from New York City, Schumer knows his voters will never catch on to the harm he is doing to the nation – the minimum wage in the City, along with Nassau, Suffolk and Westchester counties, ranges from $12 to $15 per hour, meaning his voter base is already receiving the wage he has failed to fight to bring national. Even in 2016, his constituents were making over 20% that the Federal Minimum.

But, in a climate of accepted Russian disinformation and its successful propaganda attacks of the American system, Schumer proved he was the lowest form of politician – one of those, who seeing a naked Emperor, would knowingly praise the beauty of the Emperor's New Clothes – because, rather than be honest, his goal was to please the tailor con-artists and control the simpletons.

On 9 January, Sen. Lindsey Graham suggested, *"There's a way to get what the president wants and do the least amount of damage to the country as possible. The wall plus something else* {for Democrats}."

Unfortunately, around day-20, Pelosi and Schumer met with Trump to negotiate a settlement and declared they were not going to negotiate – so Trump said "goodbye," and left. The next day, Senate Democrats demanded a Mitch McConnell allow a vote to re-open the government – with the promise that, without that vote, they would block other legislative work from proceeding.

What went unmentioned was the fact that, as Commander-in-Chief, Trump has the authority and resources to simply build the "Wall" – a fact I Blogged at 2:28AM, 13 January, and to which Trump responded with a related tweet at 10:18PM, which began, *"Border is eventually going to be militarized and defended or the United States"*.

Then too, in accordance with the language in Section 102 of the Illegal Immigration Reform and Immigrant Responsibility Act of 1996, *"The Attorney General, in consultation with the*

Commissioner of Immigration and Naturalization, shall take such actions as may be necessary to install additional physical barriers and roads (including the removal of obstacles to detection of illegal entrants) in the vicinity of the United States border to deter illegal crossings in areas of high illegal entry into the United States."

Obviously, the focus is on *"areas of high illegal entry"*, but it would appear that the Attorney General can install the "Wall" or *"additional physical barriers and roads"* without any need for consulting Congress. As his lawful boss, the President can direct the Attorney General to comply with Section 102. The only real issue would be the budgetary assignment of the cost.

CHAPTER TWO – Perception Bias
"Everything Old is New Again"

"Perception Bias" has been proven real, and it can be used to manipulate thinking. The thoughts can breed hate, or they can breed self-confidence and love. Those who oppose Trump have chosen to breed fear – to scare people into obstructing progress or anything that will ensure continuity. Satire and dark comedy are an ideal means of undermining the government, and so were used against Japan and Germany during World War Two.

Trump promotes persistence – a comical reality when seen in terms of the Feminist movement slogan: *"Nevertheless, she persisted."* But perfectly reasonable within the context of his State of the Union praise for women's advancement and Congressional representation. It is consistent with Trump's May 2004 words to students graduating Wagner College in Staten Island, where he expressed it in simple straight forward terms: *"I'll tell you, to me, the second-most important thing after love what you do is never, ever give up. Don't give up. Don't allow it to happen. If there's a concrete wall in front of you, go through it. Go over it. Go around it. But get to the other side of that wall."*

Trump speaks and thinks in terms of walls and what he told the students was really an insight into the man who became POTUS-45 and, in the usual comic fashion of history, has been spun into a reflection on "the Wall" – which, in 2004 meant the obstacles that others place in your way.

Some would have him speaking across time to the migrants – which he might well have been doing if we understand that the way past the wall was through an official gate or port of entry. But think of him speaking to Schumer and Pelosi and anyone else who would stop him from keeping his promise to those who supported his election. Look at Schumer and Pelosi as *"the concrete wall."*

Did they even stand a chance of impeding his goal?

On 19 Jan 2019 {9:09 AM}, Trump Tweeted: *"Mexico is doing NOTHING to stop the Caravan which is now fully formed and heading to the United States. We stopped the last two - many are still in Mexico but can't get through our Wall, but it takes a lot of Border Agents if there is no Wall. Not easy!"*

Was this Tweet related to the 18 January report that *"The largest single group of asylum seekers ever to cross into the US tunneled beneath the border wall near San Luis, Arizona,..."*? It is worth noting that the 376 individuals who had entered illegally via the tunnel included 176 children, 20% of whom were without either parents or guardians.

Obviously, a tunnel takes time to construct, and the lack of funding – the refusal of Pelosi and Schumer to provide adequate resources – is a major contributor to the ability of smugglers to construct tunnels. In Israel, where there are also walls, terrorists and smugglers have routinely constructed tunnels, only to have them discovered and destroyed by defense forces subsidized by the same Congress that refused to protect America's border, and, as Trump correctly pointed out, without the Wall, you need more Border Agents – whose annual cost is far greater, while their efficiency is far lower than that of a Wall.

From the standpoint of those migrants now crossing the physical Border Wall or Fence, they seem to be following Trump's advice. Those who tunneled in, they were not "captured" by any of the three agents who patrol the 26-mile-long section of the border where the crossings took place, rather the surrendered.

When interviewed, CBP Yuma Border Sector Chief Anthony Porvaznik stated that while his unit needed better border barriers – something to replace or improve upon the antiquated 12-foot metal fence – the situation was such that even greater funding was needed to provide for the migrant families, and that was becoming the priority.

As Porvaznik told the reporter, *"That's our No. 1 challenge that we have here in the Yuma sector, is the humanitarian problem. ...As I mentioned, 87 percent of the apprehensions here are family units and unaccompanied alien children."*

Of course, Congress was clearly opposed to funding either the improvements to the 2006 Secure Fence or the alternative a lack of funding was creating – the humanitarian cost of caring for the children who enter illegally and unaccompanied to become "Wards of the States."

In 2014, President Obama told Central American leaders

that migrant children entering without legitimate legal claims will be sent home. Speaking of the related influx of children in a letter to Congress, Obama stated: *"This includes fulfilling our legal and moral obligation to make sure we appropriately care for unaccompanied children who are apprehended, while taking aggressive steps to surge resources to our Southwest border to deter both adults and children from this dangerous journey, increase capacity for enforcement and removal proceedings, and quickly return unlawful migrants to their home countries."*

At the beginning of the 2014 fiscal year, Immigrant services had apprehended over 52,000 unaccompanied minors – in this context, American Immigration Lawyers Association president Leslie A. Holman viewed Obama as attempting to change the law in a manner which would *"enable the government to inflict expedited removal on unaccompanied children. That is simply unconscionable. No matter what you call it, rapid deportations without any meaningful hearing for children who are rightly afraid of the violence and turmoil from which they fled is wrong, and contradicts the fundamental values of this nation."*

Unlike Trump, who was seeking to prevent entry, Holman was inferring Obama was, without Congressional objection or media outrage, seeking to simply dump unaccompanied minors back across the border to fend for themselves or become wards of Mexico. As the 2019 Government Shutdown established, there is no interest in the Federal Government funding the care of those unaccompanied minors, and absolutely no interest in preventing the optics which encourage their parents to send them across the border.

Moreover, opposition to the Fence/Wall would seem to indicate Congress wants those children – as political pawns. Both Pelosi and Schumer apparently had good cause to want to avoid a legislative approach. Trump had used the salesman tactic of demanding the money and threatening to reject legislation which lacked it. But, theoretically, that would mean a Veto.

If we look at responsibility, it is worth noting that, as of 12 January 2019, the United States Senate website enumerated or listed all the "Vetoes by President Donald J. Trump" – a very short list, as they reported: *"President Donald J. Trump has vetoed 0 bills. There have been 2,574 1 presidential vetoes since 1789."*

That's correct, in his first two years in office, Trump had no cause to veto any passed legislation. Trump might complain, but he never vetoed. By contrast, during his term, Obama vetoed 12 legislative decision, the first being Continuing Resolution H.J. Res.64 "Continuing Appropriations, FY 2010" on 30 December 2009 – with what he termed to be a "Pocket Veto."

George W. Bush also vetoed twelve items –the first being H.R.810 the "Stem Cell Research Enhancement Act of 2005", on 19 July 2005. Bill Clinton vetoed 37 bills during his eight years in office, and George HW Bush vetoed 44 within four years.

Expressed in terms of "average" vetoes per year, Trump is proving to be a quietly purring pussycat, while George H.W. Bush was a roaring lion. Looking back further, in three years, Gerald R. Ford vetoed 66 items; looking back to Harry S Truman we see that in four-years he vetoed 250; and his predecessor/boss Franklin D. Roosevelt vetoed 635 pieces of legislation over twelve-years.

Perception is interesting. We hear the media yell all about how contentious Trump is, while Historians tend to revere FDR, whose average number of annual vetoes was 25% higher than the total for GHW Bush over four years. Transient media perception confronts historical perspective and reveals the factual bias about the way Trump works. He takes positions that cause people to avoid creating situations where real confrontation is needed.

Perception also works in the context of the 116th Congress and the Government Shutdown over was effectively funding the 2006 Secure Fence Act Nancy Pelosi opposed and Chuck Schumer originally supported when it was a victory for Obama, but then was opposed to when Donald Trump made funding its completion a campaign promise.

It is worth noting that, in March 2018, Trump had offered a solution to the DACA {'Dreamers'} problem which was tied to Border Security. At the time, referring to the Deferred Action for Childhood Arrivals program, Trump said: "*The Democrats fought us, they just fought every single inch of the way. They did not want DACA in this bill.*"

With the 2019 Government Shutdown, America saw there was no mention of DACA from either Pelosi or Schumer – but, in a televised speech on 19 January, Trump was the one who raised the issue and offered three-year protection for DACA, which should have been ample time for the House to frame permanent legislation. From a political point of view, it is more important to note that, if Pelosi believe the Democrats had a shot at the White House in 2020, she would have jumped at the chance to accept Trumps offer to tie Fence funding to the Bridge Act, which would protect undocumented individuals who came to the united states as children.

In 2017, Democrats were willing to fund about $25 Billion, in exchange for retaining "chained migration" and a "catch-and-release" policy which returned those who entered illegally to the streets while their cases were adjudicated – which, due to the combined effect of underfunding and short staffing was a process that could take years.

The message being sent was that immigration and border security laws were effectively meaningless – something affirmed on 19 November 2018, when Judge Jon Tigar, of the U.S. District Court for the Northern District of California, ruled that "The [Administrative] rule barring asylum for immigrants who enter the country outside a port of entry irreconcilably conflicts with the INA and the expressed intent of Congress." In effect, Judge Tigar declared that those who circumvented lawful points of entry would receive the same treatment as those who obeyed the law, criminal behavior was, therefore, to be rewarded.

It is a simple matter of Border Security which was proved effective by the sharp decline in apprehensions after completion of the authorized first 650-miles of the structure. In terms of bias, what is interesting is that, on 3 January, the first day of the 116th Congress and 12-days after the Shutdown over $5.7 Billion in funding for the remaining phase of the 2006 law, the New Congress introduced legislation titled: "*Strengthening America's Security in the Middle East Act of 2019.*"

Reading the act {S.1, TITLE I, Subtitle A, SEC. 111:7}, then revealed it sought an appropriation of $3.3 Billion annually, for a period of ten years, totaling $33 billion American taxpayer dollars to effectively construct and/or maintain a Border Security Wall, for Israel. As important as Israel is to the America presence in the Middle East, one would suspect America could afford to spend ten-percent as much to fund its own existing domestic security law and needs.

Of course, it should be pointed out that, when Senators Schumer, Obama, and Clinton signed on to the 2006 Secure Fence Act, they were doing so knowing they were making a $50 Billion commitment to border security which would extend over a 25-year period – so into the 2031 era associated with the predicted Third World War.

On an annual basis, the commitment to Israel is roughly fifty-percent higher, but they would be in the center of the ignition point for the next World War, so the extra cost is reasonable. The issue is now the desire to effectively open the Southern border to the wave of individuals who are and will be, driven north by the combined effects of Climate Change, economic collapse, and Civil Wars in South and Central America.

How about China, and North Korea, would they seek some form of NAFTA – which Trump had renegotiated into the United States–Mexico–Canada Agreement {USMCA}?

Wouldn't it be funny if both wanted the same appearance, but for diametrically different reasons? The Disruptive Actor is one who uses criticism to undermine the authority and validity of any action, while meaningless disruption can also serve to distract those who are hell-bent on serious disruption. Criticism can be a tool for improvement, distraction, and disruption. For Trump, it formed a basis for promoting his brand – the ultimate criticism and reward being "You're Fired!"

If someone wishes to find to criticize, a basis can always be found or invented. If you want action or a situation to carry a negative connotation – doing so is rather easy, and is a favorite among those who are disruptive or socially destructive. For this reason, we saw Ted Cruz represent the far-Right-wing types with his call to repeal Obamacare; then saw Trump brush Cruz aside by calling for repeal through replacement with an improved, more universal, healthcare alternative of the type existing in Australia.

The 2018 Midterm election, showed Texas preferred Cruz. But, when it comes to actual implementation of the law, a Senator is subordinate to a Governor, and across the nation, Red States decided they preferred Blue Governors. In Maine, immediately upon election, Democrat Janet Mills said top priorities as Maine's next governor would be expanding Medicaid, and lowering health insurance premiums. It was a sentiment echoed across the nation.

You need only decide, or, as shown in *The Emperor's New Clothes*, once told what to see, it shall be seen by those who seek the approval of others, by those who want to "fit in." That runs into problems when someone who was either not told or doesn't care to be part of the "crowd" reveals what really is. It is then, at that point, that the "simpleton masses" decide to either blindly follow or actually think about what is right before their eyes.

Two days after the Midterm election, The Washington Post reported the next stage in the surrender of the Right-wing, which was already seen when Ted Cruz "bent a knee" to Trump and thus received the backing he needed to win re-election.

As the Post put it: "*For eight years, Republicans waged a war against Barack Obama's health-care law, holding dozens of repeal votes, filing lawsuits and branding it a dangerous government takeover.*" A Day after the election, "*they effectively surrendered,*" because the Democrats now controlled the House and with that control came an end to any legislative repeal. More important, the Republicans lost Governors who had been blocking Medicare expansion.

Through their loss, Trump had won a clear opportunity to expand his legacy to include the creation of the best healthcare system in the world. If that were to happen, Trump's Evangelical supporters would finally be on the right side of Scriptures and moving away from being the ongoing butt of Saint Paul's joke.

Any competent salesman, propagandist or hypnotist both knows and relies upon control of, "Perception Bias". Nobody will do anything they are not instinctively inclined to do, therefore it is important to phrase things in a manner that triggers inherent response in a way that redirects it to make the sale, gets the vote, or in any other way gets the audience to gladly experience the act of obedience to a suggestion or command.

In *The Emperor's New Clothes*, the beauty of the clothes described was allegedly evidence of a high-IQ and the means by which the viewer became securely ensconced among the majority or "in-crowd." By denouncing alleged "criminal activities" – the groundwork having been laid with Benghazi – Trump was able to invoke a preconditioned response to Hillary Clinton. However, since the response mindset was broadly established, immediately upon victory, his opposition used the identical tactic on him.

A magician will do the same thing, use the technique, but focus only on changing the visual perception, where others change thoughts, and rely upon the masses being traditional simpletons, willing to set aside logic, rationality, and dismiss any evidence derived from experience or their own eyes. Climate denial is yet another example. The melting glaciers and ice caps which cause rising sea levels which flood low-lying islands and coastal land masses are clear evidence of global warming.

We now know that the techniques, propaganda techniques developed and perfected since 1956, are being used on the internet by bots and trolls to spread various misinformation about political candidates and also appears in the anti-vaxxer movement which serves to establish a basis for the spread of preventable diseases.

The anti-vaxxer movement would be related to the attacks on Obamacare, Medicare, and all other health-related issues – it would also include the anti-abortion movement, which is designed to increase deaths among women and push the poor further into poverty. This is underscored by the anti-abortion demand of no abortion, even in the case of an Ectopic Pregnancy which can kill or render the mother infertile, and so murder all the children she might have had – two-percent of all pregnancies are Ectopic, and as women delay childbearing the percentage grows rapidly.

Supreme Court nominee Brett Kavanaugh has apparently pointed the Constitution does not mention abortion. Of course, it does not mention the fetus at all and recognizes existence only when a person is born. Therefore, it would follow that a fetus is the legal equivalent of a tumor – a cellular growth whose DNA is defined by both host and foreign elements. Therefore treatment is determined by the woman and her doctor; the government has no Constitutional right to interject itself into the use of traditional medically approved and supervised treatments.

Of course, during the confirmation hearing, Kavanaugh was asked by Senator Kamala Harris (D-CA), *"Can you think of any laws that give government the power to make decisions about the male body?"* It was an interesting question, especially if its logic was applied to actual laws – in which case it would mean that Senator Harris either wanted to legalize female circumcision or outlaw male circumcision since both represent legislative control over one gender rather than uniform gender-specific treatment.

Harris' mother is Tamil Indian, so she might well have been looking to the possibility of legalizing female circumcision – which is also called "female genital mutilation," and is practiced in India, where it is legal. On the other hand, there is the possibility Harris was contemplating making the religious practice of circumcision – which is also medically recommended to prevent the transfer of HIV and other STD's – illegal. In either case, Harris could have been testing whether a gender bias argument would pass muster with Kavanagh as a SCOTUS justice.

George Washington University scientists discovered trolls and bots, with origins in Russia, were skewing online debate and upending consensus about vaccine safety. These same Russian trolls have been connected to efforts to interfere with both sides in the 2016 election. Their efforts are not aimed at promoting one side or point of view, rather the goal is to create a level of discord which will serve to fracture the society – it is also now known that Russia promoted the BREXIT movement which, in 2018, was seen to be undermining the British economy.

In September 2017, FaceBook claimed it closed several hundred accounts linked to the Kremlin. But that had no effect on the propaganda Trolls on either FaceBook, Instagram, or any Social Media platforms. Later reports indicated Troll accounts reaching 300,000 Americans; this can be placed in the context of a House Intelligence Committee report asserting the intent was to create or exacerbate divisions in American society. But these efforts are not confined to America, rather they appear on a range of social media in numerous nations where it would benefit Russia to sow division and discord with narratives calling for Donald Trump's impeachment while speculating on criminal activity for which no specifics or evidence was produced.

In January 2019, House Intelligence Committee Chairman Adam Schiff, D-Calif said of impeachment, "*What's the point if you don't know the full case and can't make the case to the Senate?*" But those seeking to undermine the government do not require any evidence, they do not need facts, they have negative propaganda.

In a study published by Clint Watts on 16 January 2018, we are told: *"Within the Kremlin's playbook, each social media platform serves a function, a role in an interlocking social media ecosystem where Russia infiltrates, engages, influences and manipulates targeted American audiences."*

The Russians are using a practical application of the attack Nikita Khrushchev boasted he would employ to allow the United States to defeat itself. Based on the timing, it is possible Russia was behind or derived its methodology from the ease by which he saw Senator Joseph McCarthy echo Hitler's anti-Semitic actions become a "Red Scare" that contaminated the term "socialism" and allowed McCarthyism to take control of various segments of the culture. Of course, that was also the era in which Ronald Reagan converted from Roosevelt Democrat to Conservative Republican and, like many in Hitler's Germany, spying on his neighbors and co-workers in the entertainment industry in the service of the House Un-American Activities Committee [HUAC].

Over the next seventy years, the social discord process was refined and perfected by observing the natural dissident process as the model for each nation under attack, The primary objective is to focus on those who are easiest to reach.

Climate Change denial is an example of what is happening. It began by targeting regions where the effects were least visible and, therefore, was an easy sell. This allowed construction of an acceptance base which could then be expanded. It follows they would target the Bible Belt or Midwestern Evangelical Christians, who blindly accept fallacies such as our calendar year one being the year when Jesus was born, even though we know he was about three when Herod died, and Herod died 4-years prior to the first year of our calendar, and about 3-years after the Biblical birth and 2-years after the family migrated to Egypt.

People will believe anything, accordingly, when the United Nations issued its October Climate Report, the Republican leaders denounced it. The Intergovernmental Panel on Climate Change {IPCC} determination that, relative to pre-industrial levels, the related greenhouse gas emission will drive global warming up by 2.7 degrees Fahrenheit (1.5 degrees Celsius) between 2030 and

2052 – so Republicans like Louisiana Senator John Kennedy said: *"That's the problem with the U.N., that they come up with these policy ideas that are just 'La La Land'."*

In *'La La land'* major coastal metropolises like New York City will be subject to calamitous flooding. And Florida Senator Marco Rubio was unconcerned with the prospect of the major part of his state being underwater and, could not seem to make the connection to conditions which would then exist when another Hurricane Michael (which destroyed parts of his state as he spoke) would have even far worse consequences.

Compiled by 91 scientists from 40 countries who analyzed more than 6,000 scientific studies, the IPCC report pointed to an era of worsening food shortages and wildfires, with a mass die-off of coral reefs as soon as 2040.

But, like most politicians, Kennedy and Rubio cannot think in terms beyond the next coming election or election cycles they will be a part of. Thinking twelve years ahead is far beyond their feeble mental abilities – or those of the "Dump Trump" legions we see pushing to undermine the Constitution and government.

All politicians play to the native beliefs of their voter base – it's the easiest way to acquire elective power. In previous books on Trump administration and methodology, with an eye toward the nature of the base Trump now commands, I quoted Hitler's words from his 1924 bestseller, *Mein Kampf*: *"Propaganda is a truly terrible weapon in the hands of an expert."*

The truth of Hitler's observation was brought home to the far-Right-wing when Trump simply walked in and took over the base they had been cultivating for decades. A part of what Trump does is first appear to accept the dominant false premise and then introduce a shift in terminology.

With both Climate Change and the Obama Birth Certificate Birther issue, he prefaced things with "experts tell me." Thus, he appears to accept the topic, while he is actually saying he's accepting the words of someone else. This means the facts used by the "experts" can later be challenged with the introduction of superior logical or rational analysis supported by real, better, or more accurate facts.

Looking at the climate denial debate, we see it evolved from the idea there was no change – refuted by temperature readings dating back 100-years – to one which argues human activity is not the cause of the changes – which is refuted by the parallel climb of population and temperature which includes temperature drops concurrent with wars and plagues in industrialized nations.

How does Trump approach Climate Change? He suggests the southern border wall/fence have solar collectors; he knows coal usage is declining, and he speaks of "clean coal" technology, which represents a technology that is very important to China and Japan. It also represents a strategic benefit to the United States, in the event of another OPEC Oil Embargo, or the final depletion of America's limited oil reserves being drained by Fracking.

The disbelief in a slow environmental change that is unseen by most people is an easy thing to manipulate; so, we should not be surprised when a percentage of the population denies evolution and climate change. Hitler termed them *"The Simpleton Masses"* and recognized how easily the British had manipulated them in the First World War. What we now know, from research into the subject, is that, if you can convince a quarter of the population, the whole population will fall into line.

As presented in the 2017 Trump Card book series, Hitler's quote leads to: *"THE EMPEROR'S NEW CLOTHES is a classic tale of how people will ignore the evidence of their own eyes, ignore reality, rather than face the condemnation of others too fearful of public opinion to address reality. It is mob psychology of the form which enables the trickster to control and make fools of average people."*

On Monday, 10 December 2018, the UN climate summit heard of the urgent need to phase out of all coal burning and thus help cut carbon emissions; as a counterpoint, only a week before, it was reported that Poland was expanding its reliance on coal. A key point that was made was purely economic – without the cuts, the world would face a financial crash several times worse than the 2008 crisis.

As we know, the K-WAVE pattern analysis, which has been accurate over a 200-year period, is predicting a crash in 2027. This argues the high probability of a world likely to follow the Polish model, while economic leaders, such as California, are beginning to require that, by 2020, all new home construction and structures of less than three stories include solar collectors as part of their basic design.

As we know, the impact of climate change can be sudden, severe and catastrophic – as was seen with the "Camp Fire" and related fires which decimated California in the fall of 2018. Given the new analysis, if Trump really is financially capable, and has amassed wealth by skill and not dumb luck, we will see him take a track that actively encourages the job and economic growth that is a primary characteristic of a renewable energy industry which shall also free the nation of the national security threat of Saudi and Russian oil being cut.

Climate Change is one example of what the Republicans have been doing since Reagan, and Creationist thinking predates Reagan by two centuries and refuses to succumb to intelligence, rationality, or the genetics of propagation described in the Bible – a book proponents of ignorance consistently misrepresent, and those who profess to believe in wisdom choose to ignore.

Trump has taken advantage of Republican ignorance and used it to slowly "turn the stampeding herd." Naturally, the herd does not realize it's being turned. Nor do they realize that attacks on him serve his purpose. Spectators scream against him while running in the very direction he wants them to go. Remember, he needs to attain or maintain that 25-percent acceptance threshold in a herd that is composed of confused masses stampeding toward the cliff.

ALL leaders are, by definition, dictatorial — they command their followers to follow, and expect obedience. But initially, they must be acknowledged as the leader. When that occurs, they can lead their herd to peace and safety, or into the depths of war and hardship. Until there is an unquestioned leader, it is the mindless acts of the herd which determines their fate. Both the Jihadists and Evangelicals are awaiting an undisputed leader, and then the fun begins in earnest.

When the herd is stampeding, its leader generally leads by following from the front. That is, they see where the stampeding herd is going and run with it to position themselves at its head; it is only then that they can be recognized and assume control.

It is the classic wisdom contained in an anecdote about the early days of the French Revolution and Robespierre who is said to have been sitting at a Paris café with friends when a mob passes heading in the direction of the prison known as the Bastille.

Someone says: "Who are those people and where are they going?" To which another person says: "Just a mob of peasants – looks like they're headed for the Bastille."

Robespierre gulps his wine, jumps from his seat and starts after them. His friend calls out: "Where are you going?"

Robespierre shouts back: "With them!"

And his friend calls out: "Why are you running?"

"I must to the front of them!"

"Why?"

To which Robespierre shouts: "Because I'm their leader!"

As any lead stallion knows, before you can begin to turn the stampeding herd, you must be seen as its leader. For that to happen, you must first go where the herd is already headed – in politics, you tell the people to go where they are already going to go anyway. When they come to believe you are simply telling them to do what they were going to would have done anyway, they cease to think about what you are telling them to do – and simply follow your directions.

It is only at that point, that the lead stallion gets to turn the stampeding herd, or political leaders get to establish a new policy. Unlike Warren, Sanders, or any of the Right-wing stars, Trump is in the business of turning the herd by having them make the clear decision to turn. As a result, as we will see, individuals like Senator Schumer tend to be caught forcefully arguing against the positions they built their careers promoting.

This is one of the horrors of the current transitional "Post-Truth" era which became visible on a global level in 2016, when Trump was elected because the Electoral College functioned and the British again asserted their self-destructive ways through the populist BREXIT vote which would separate their economy from that of the European Union an set the stage for a downward spiral that could bring about an Economic Depression predicted by the Kondratiev-Wave {K-Wave} long economic cycle analysis which was revealed by Soviet economist Nikolai Kondratiev in his 1925 book, *The Major Economic Cycles*.

As we have covered in the previous Trump Card books in this series, as a businessman, Trump to disengage America while also creating a global balance between the United States and the reemerging and modernized Chinese mercantile culture which was once historically known as *"The Silk Road."*

In 2019, rather than rely on silkworms and spices, China is building upon American intellectual property to create a 21st-century high-tech renewable energy economy. To be part of that, Trump has entered into the negotiations with Beijing, while also working to assist Kim Jong-un in transforming North Korea into a mercantile hub or Asia intermediary.

On striking aspect of the "Post-Truth Era" is its traditional roots in the facts that Politicians lie and news reporting is biased. The difference is that, in the United States, we now see those liars and distorters of reality pointing at Trump for using PT Barnum techniques – in many cases, using what we can call plagiarism, but which is actually the traditional technique of using an opponents words against them. In this way, when the timing is right, you need only quote your opponent – or, in the modern age, contrast the video of them using the very arguments you "plagiarized" to further their objectives, and then later attacking their own points and words when you express them to achieve the identical goal.

We saw trump use this in a 15 August 2018 Tweet, where he attached the words "Chuck Schumer, I agree!" to a video of a 2009 speech in which Senator Chuck Schumer explicitly stated: *"Illegal immigration is wrong, plain and simple."*

A C-SPAN video from 14 MAY 2014, shows Senator Chuck Schumer attacking House Republicans for behaving exactly as House Democrats behaved in December 2018. And we have the 9 November 2015 pro-wall words of Hillary Clinton asserting: *"I voted numerous times when I was a senator to spend money to build a barrier to try to prevent illegal immigrants from coming in."*

CHAPTER THREE – SOCIALIST

"A man is a success if
he gets up in the morning and
goes to bed at night and
in between does what he wants to do."
~ Bob Dylan

What is it that we, as a society and culture, want?

Since the 1960s, Nikita Khrushchev has been given credit for asserting:

"We will take America without firing a shot... We will BURY YOU! We can't expect the American People to jump from Capitalism to Communism, but we can assist their elected leaders in giving them small doses of Socialism until they awaken one day to find that they have Communism. We do not have to invade the United States, we will destroy you from within."

There is no dated source for the words and they sound like a combination of phrases dating back to the days of Lenin. Still, they do reflect a reality we like to ignore – Socialism is an inherent quality within humans and is traditional to cultures or religions, as seen embodied in the Biblical *"You shall love your neighbor as yourself."*

That verse, attributed to Jesus, appears in Matthew 22:39 but comes from Jesus' teacher, Rabbi Hillel, who, when asked to summarize all of Torah while standing on one leg, said: *"That which is hateful unto you do not do to your neighbor."*

As can be observed in American society, there are many in both the Right and Left of the political spectrum who take great pride in helping their neighbor whenever it will cause far greater harm to the overall society. The controversy over the border wall falls into this area – migrants are to receive free food, clothing, shelter, and medical care denied or objected to when provided to citizens. This becomes an issue where Socialism for migrants who illegally enter America is fine, but it is not something to fight for if the recipient is a native-born or naturalized citizen.

Instead of opposing Trump's Wall – which is basically what Senator Chuck Schumer sponsored and promoted in his June 2013 legislation – both Schumer and House Speaker Nancy Pelosi should be fighting for programs Bernie Sanders has advocated. No rational person could doubt that President Trump would sign legislation that would bolster his legacy and much of what Sanders advocates would do just that.

However, impeding the nation's growth, so as to damage any Trump Presidential Legacy, seems to be the secondary aspect of the propaganda attacks which began in November 2016. For some reason, America and much of the Western World ceased being rational in 2016 – as shown by the June 2016 BREXIT vote.

In 1964, Khrushchev declared that *"The press is our chief ideological weapon."* And this was true until the Internet and its Social Media component replaced print as the weapon of choice – in propaganda terms, it introduced a nuclear weapon and placed it in the hands of children.

Shakespeare's *Othello*, with its various elements of racism, betrayal, variations on inappropriate sexual behavior, which are joined with bigotry derived violence and murder, serve as a solid platform for the necessary propaganda.

Othello was a Venetian Moor – an olive-skinned or a dark complexioned African Muslim who could be based on his origin, be placed in the same conceptional context of bigotry visited upon Shylock in *'The Merchant of Venice.'*

Both works came into existence concurrent with the first American colonies. The ideas they present, the bigotry, served to define the first four-hundred years of what is now known as the United States. These roots are both the antithesis of Socialism, and Biblical values – even while the Bible was being used to justify the bigotry. That is, it was, and is still, used indirect manipulation to promote hate. In the process we see Nazis and neo-Nazis use it to attack Jews – ignoring the fact that Jesus and all the Apostles were devout Jews. This means they are symbolically encouraging their followers to murder Jesus – and it one believes in the second coming, to murder him prior to his announcing his return.

Karl Marx was a Jew who taught Jewish Socialism of a type practiced by the Essenes, but with the addition of Capitalism in a form that allowed "surplus capital" to be devoted to the common good. Communism, as practiced by Lenin was different from that imposed by Stalin, which is different from that associated with those who subsequently called themselves Communists rather than the dictators they really are.

As mentioned in "*Jonathon's POTUS Cousins*," Karl Marx promoted Capitalism – with the fall of Soviet Communism, Russia and China can be viewed as Capitalist nations that are more in line with the Marxist concept.

At it's heart, Biblical Socialism, as expressed in the design of the Twelve Tribes; the mandate to Tithe 10-percent of earnings, or as much of that amount as can be provided without inflicting hardship on yourself and your family; the idea that the Merchant Tribe (class) should fully support the Scholar's Tribe (which also included full support for their families); plus care and support for the sick, orphaned, and aged, is all pure socialism.

The goal of socialism, the type of society portrayed in the TV series STAR TREK, is to allow the individual to do what they love – to follow their heart. So it is that the character of Benjamin Lafayette Sisko – Star Trek: Deep Space Nine (DS9) – enters Star Fleet, while his father, Joseph Sisko, can take pride in being a New Orleans, Creole chef, and owner of "Sisko's Creole Kitchen, at a time when a replicator can provide, and does provide, food.

It is noteworthy that nobody who has watched the series ever saw a "Sisko's" patron pay – because the food is free – Joseph is, like others in the Federation, doing what they love; it is only in the alien societies that we see greed and slavery.

Only those who oppose the Bible would take no issue with those who oppose its socialistic ideals – in America, this means those associated with the Right-wing and others who only use the Bible as a bludgeon to support their bigotry and hate.

There are three basic economic cultures which comprise a triangular base for an economic pyramid – the peak of which is where they come together: Individual Capitalism; Slavery, and old testament Golden Rule-based economics which, in modern times, became known as either Marxism or Socialism.

Karl Marx was producing his economic theories in 1840, a time period that is important to the concept he was espousing. It is equally important to recognize he did so from the vantage point of a Hebrew scholar presenting Biblical Economic Theory.

In his era, Religion was a means of repression and justified a subjugation of people – just as today it is used to support racism and bigotry in America against those born homosexual, and in the Middle East as a basis for the mass murder of innocents in the name of Jihad. Curiously, both the Bible and Koran use prophecy to tell us this will culminate in a World War in sometime around 2035. Marx understood the inevitability of the conflict between human morality and religious bigotry, so he could not state he was using the Bible as his basis.

Still, in his preface to the first German edition of *"Capital, A Critique of Political Economy"* {1867}, he looks back to the Old Testament period when he tells the reader he is popularizing the analysis of the substance and magnitude of value or the form it takes in society, by saying:

> *"The value-form, whose fully developed shape is the money-form, is very elementary and simple. Nevertheless, the human mind has for more than 2,000 years sought in vain to get to the bottom of it all,..."*

Apart from various social and moral negatives promoted by organized religion, which justifies adopting an agnostic approach – that approach being to reject organized religion while avoiding the core issue of a Creator or source of the Universe which would yield something from absolute nothing. If one says the Universe is eternal, then the Universe is God – or, as the Egyptians phrased it, came about as a self-begotten beginning. Marx simply accepted higher levels of universal morality in terms of observable reality. He, therefore, is free to speak of the economic benefit we all derive from common ownership of those valuable resources or capital assets, which serve everyone.

In modern society, we could look at Government Buildings, roads, bridges, schools, hospitals, and even clean energy sources or any other asset which people need and use on a routine basis.

Marx refers to "Surplus-Value" generated by the individual and which he refers to in interesting terms: *"The Relation of the Rate of Surplus-Value to the Rate of Profit, which treats the subject mathematically (in equations)."* As he phrased it, and in his various notes, papers, and writings, he appears to be speaking of what, since 1913, Americans have called Income Tax.

In part IV of *Das Kapital*, Marx presents his equation in words which describe the capitalist system which generates the surplus value. He speaks in terms of a standard workday, which did not exist in his day, and then of overtime hours *"Beyond this necessary labor-time."* As we would recognize today, he needs to inform his readers, *"The rate of surplus-value and the length of the working day depended on the length of this extension. Although the necessary labor-time was constant, the total working day was variable."*

In an era that had no standard 35 or 40 hour week, Marx posits it as a hypothetical: *"Now suppose a working day with a given length and division between necessary labor and surplus labor."* In his era, he needed to speak of the norm his audience would recognize: *"for example, a working day of 12 hours ... 10 hours of necessary labor, and ... 2 hours of surplus labor."* He then expresses the problem, how to increase the production of surplus-value or surplus labor, without prolonging the work day.

In an age of slavery, Marx was addressing the problem of increased productivity which would then produce the funds that could then be "taxed" and used to used to benefit the masses. As he said, *"It would not be the length of the working day that changes, but its division into necessary labor-time and surplus labor-time."*

Obviously, Marx is speaking in economic terms that were a century before their time and we can continue to translate his 19th century concept into the reality of the 21st century, but we can shorthand it by saying he was talking about increasing efficiency, while maintaining earnings and increasing the Gross Domestic Product {GDP} by increasing worker pay in a manner consistent with increases in production efficiency. An early experiment with implementing this idea was "piecework" – pay workers for items produced rather than hours worked.

Marx died at the age of 64, on 14 March 1883, just five days after the death of 30-year old English economic historian Arnold Toynbee, who is credited with defining the nature and meaning of the Industrial Revolution. As an Oxford professor, he taught his

Indian students that "*they should learn Political Economics after the old fashion, but that the theory must be applied to an Oriental or semi-civilized country – with a difference.*" {from "Lectures on the Industrial Revolution in England," published posthumously with a memoir by B. Jowett}

As we see from the memoir quote, we have an element of what can be considered an economic equivalent of Einstein's theory relativity. Concepts of Free Trade that were normal in Europe, when dealing a different culture, were not to be taken as fixed; Free Trade was no advantageous when the basic economic systems were different. It is the recognition of this which America saw when President Trump declared prior trade agreements bad deals for America.

The reader learns that those preaching the accumulation of wealth, also left the distribution to take care of itself. In modern terms, he was describing Reagan's "Trickle Down Economics" and Trumps 2018 Tax Reform, which failed to include an increase in both Minimum Wage and average Social Security – both of which, when annualized, are half of poverty and therefore place a burden on taxpayers in the form of Public Assistance, rather than place the burden on consumers to support those who provide goods and services they actually use.

Effectively, the system is engineered to tax non-Wal-Mart customers – generally urban dwellers – so they can subsidize both the owners of Wal-Mart and rural America. The true effect is to remove real income from rural areas and therefore to force them onto the poverty rolls. Were the foundational income raised to 150% of poverty levels and pegged to automatically increase in line with an increase in the poverty threshold, rural communities would enjoy prosperity and increased wealth. But this would have the political effect of undermining Right-wing rants which focus on city dwelling "Welfare Queens." For that reason, on November first, just five days before the election, Larry Kudlow, the director of Donald Trump's National Economic Council, asserted, "My view is a federal minimum wage is a terrible idea. A terrible idea," adding, "I would argue against state and local, but that's up to the states and localities."

Do away with the minimum wage and you force an increase in the welfare numbers, and that provides campaign fodder that relies on attacking welfare as the cause of deficits. The real goal is, of course, to force the nation into bankruptcy by removing as much disposable income as possible from the economic equation.

However, the Republicans love people to be poor, which we can say explains why, for the past 40-years, the *"productivity-pay gap"* has expanded. What this reflects is the fact that, since 1973, there had been a 77-percent increase in American productivity, but hourly pay grew only 12 percent. Had the Federal Minimum Wage kept pace, the poverty wage of $7.25 would now be closer to $20/hour.

Bernie Sanders has suggested the minimum be raised to $15/hour. Trump inherited an economy in which nearly a third of the American worker – about 41.7 million blue-collar types— earn less than $12 an hour. Sanders wants a 25% increase for workers who should be getting a 75% raise, while the Republicans fight to reduce the Federal Supplement represented by Public Assistance paid to about 18.25% of the "working poor." Phrased another way, about 60% of the poor are in households where at least one person has a job.

Public Assistance is either paid for by current taxes, or by debit to be paid with future taxes on a smaller population base. In the case of Social Security, the cost, which must be immediately paid, comes from a dedicated tax; unlike infrastructure, it cannot be deferred until sometime when structures collapse and people die. Those on Social Security vote and they will get angry – many were Hippies; they opposed Vietnam and changed the culture – They still oppose those they opposed sixty years ago and they are winning, as we saw with the continued support for Bernie Sanders and the election of Alexandria Ocasio-Cortez.

An increase in Social Security could be covered by simply raising the contribution Social Security Wage Base cap, which, in 2018 was $128,400 – with both employee and employer paying 6.20% of income – to $256,800, with further increases pegged to annual inflation. Given the Baby-Boom demographics, and best possible average global life expectancy, this would create a slight surplus to offset the National Debt growth, and after 2045 there could be sufficient surplus to buy back all foreign-held debt.

If it were done properly, and the Legislature waited for the reduced a subsequent final budget report to show actual savings realized in Public Assistance. Such savings could fund a national wind, solar, or geothermal energy program to propel the United States ahead of China and European nations moving away from dependence on Middle Eastern oil and fossil fuels in general.

This would lower energy costs and, by the restructuring of the easily targeted centralized primary grid networks, increase national security. The grid would still exist, but only to distribute surplus energy.

America is still fighting against the 19th century Poor Law that we all know from the workhouse Dickens mentioned in "A Christmas Carol".

Passed concurrent with the end of slavery in England in 1834, the Poor Laws helped assure the poor the freedom of labor, but, they offered no access to education or chance to emigrate, so had the effect of trapping people in their original place of abode – under ordinary conditions, this meant they the liberty to starve.

With Social Security, Food Stamps, and other programs, many of the failings of the Poor Law were remedied. Reaganomics and "Workfare" were the first step in putting the government into the business of subsidizing private sector wage slavery.

While not wage slavery, or anything that would contribute to closing the "productivity-pay gap", it is worth noting that, on 30 August, President Trump announced:

> *"I have determined that for 2019, both across the board pay increases and locality pay increases will be set at zero. These alternative pay plan decisions will not materially affect our ability to attract and retain a well qualified Federal workforce. We must maintain efforts to put our Nation on a fiscally sustainable course, and Federal agency budgets cannot sustain such increases."*

With that announcement, the prospect of a 25.7% raise for localities and a general rise of 2.1% came to an end.

Percentages and statistics are boring, which explains why the media tends to avoid examining the underlying data before branding something false or a lie. It is also why pundits often misrepresent statistics – they know people are unlikely to verify the analysis. A case in point is the focus on atmospheric gases when talking about Climate Change.

While it is true that these gases are directly linked to the climate change problem, the reality is that they exist because of population growth, and grow in direct proportion to population growth. Understanding this, but realizing it is too complex for the average person to grasp, we saw Trump dismiss the Paris Climate Accord.

On 27 February 219, an article on Alexandria Ocasio-Cortez reported: *"On Instagram, the congresswoman said millennials are choosing to be childless because of the climate crisis."*

The Guardian article went on to posit a question which reflects the causal reality: *"Alexandria Ocasio-Cortez, freshman congresswoman and social media sensation, has taken time out from baiting Donald Trump and establishment members of her own party to raise a profound moral question for us all: in light of the escalating climate emergency, should we still be having children?"*

However, the question AOC posited on Instagram showed she really didn't understand there is a causal connection between population growth and resulting change in global temperatures: *"It is basically a scientific consensus that the lives of our children are going to be very difficult, and it does lead young people to have a legitimate question: is it OK to still have children?"*

The article went on to reference the fact that there was a study which connected population to climate change and advised one less child per family. Phrased another way, families should stop at two children – because an average of 2.1 children defines Zero Population Growth (ZPG). Since not everyone reproduces, traditional families, which we now associate with the Republican reference to those post-war families of the Baby-Boom era, have had more than three children.

A 2007 Lancet paper estimated, "Nearly half of the global population is less than 25 years old 1."

If they adhered to pre-modern fertility rates, every female (nearly one-quarter of the global population) would eventually have an average of 4.5 to 7 children. After the Second World War, and in conjunction with the Baby-Boom, the expansion of modern medicine prevented early deaths and extended longevity. As a result, the need for high reproduction rates declined – had they not, there would have been an exponential growth and eventually climate change would kill all life on the planet.

But, because children now survive to adulthood, parents recognized the could have fewer children, with the added benefit of gaining a higher standard of living without jeopardizing their family's multi-generational survival. As a result, global fertility rates fell from a 1950-1955 rate of 4.96 to 2.52 in 2010–2015. In 2019, it was estimated that the 2015-2020 rate would approach 2.11.

Reports during the first two months of 2019, estimated the replacement rate had already passed below 2.1, with the prognoses it would remain there. This means an extended period of Negative Population Growth {NPG}.

For those who accept the predictions in Revelation – either as some scientific knowledge we have yet to understand or divine prophesy – the reality is, Climate Change related death of multiple life-forms, combined with NPG, and the death of the Baby-Boom generation by 2050, will cause the fulfillment of the prophecy of a third of "life" dying-off in the mid-21st-century.

In terms of Socialism, support for Universal Medicare or National Health Services creates a means of combating Climate Change – by lowering infant mortality, while also extending life expectancy, and thereby reducing the need for a high fertility rate.

If we look at the basic platform proposed by Bernie Sanders and AOC, we see basic Universal Healthcare and above poverty Minimum Wages as their core. In terms of solid economics, these make total sense and are completely logical – just as they were in the age of Jesus when he told the story of the Good Samaritan.

Given that Trump, Sanders, and AOC have each supported some form of an improved healthcare system, we can be reasonably confident they would all agree with the words of PT Barnum as expressed in his *"Golden Rules for Making Money"*, and quoted in the first book in this series – *"No Trump Card"*:

"In the United States, where we have more land than people, it is not at all difficult for persons in good health to make money."

"The foundation of success in life is good health: that is the

substratum fortune; it is also the basis of happiness. A person cannot accumulate a fortune very well when he is sick."

It is worth repeating the conclusion, based on those quoted words, *"Only those who want America to fail, those who want Donald to fail, both as a President and as a World Leader, would oppose ensuring Americans have the best healthcare system in the world."*

Consistent with much of what we hear from both Sanders and AOC – and often see in Trump's deeds, though not in his words, Barnum also denounced what we now call the 1%, those he simply referred to as "misers", as well as Evangelical and Pence connected Religious bigots and demagogues:

"...misers who hoard money only for the sake of hoarding and who have no higher aspiration than to grasp everything which comes within their reach. As we have sometimes hypocrites in religion, and demagogues in politics, so there are occasionally misers among money-getters."

As we know, the "Dump Trump" movement began Election night 2016, with only one discernable goal, that is, the installation of Might Pence and the Ultra Right-wing in the Oval Office. That would empower both the "demagogues" and "hypocrites," while ensuring the denial of healthcare to any of those seeking success for themselves of their posterity.

As we know, FoxNews is an anti-Socialist, anti-American champion – but we would need to look to House Speaker Nancy Pelosi and Senator Chuck Schumer to see an introduction of both demagogue and hypocrite into the mix. While we will discuss both Pelosi and Schumer later, for now, let's look at Fox News.

On 18 August 2018, FoxNews' Trish Ragan made a massive mistake and decided to proclaim *"There's Something Rotten in Denmark"* and, when Social Democrat Dan Jorgensen responded, she got her butt kicked.

First off, she made the mistake of claiming "Denmark, like Venezuela has stripped people of their opportunity". Denmark is, of course, one of the homelands of the Vikings, the earliest and most successful socialist mercantile warrior cultures in history. It was a Social Democratic nation a millennia before the political terms came into existence.

Jorgensen replied, Denmark provides opportunities for its people; he didn't mention that they live the culture preached in the Bible, he only enumerated the elements of that culture. It was pointed out that, in terms of work, the Organization for Economic Co-operation and Development (OECD) ranked Denmark higher than the United States.

In unemployment the USA, even with the record lows of the Trump administration, still ranks 19th versus Denmark's 8th – six months later, Denmark's unemployment rate stood at 3.7%, the lowest it had been since February 2009, and America was at 3.9% with an estimated up-tick to 4%.

In addition, as Bernie Sanders advocated after the election, in Denmark, all the Universities are Free and student's receive living cost – Regan believed this meant nobody would work, but it does, probably, explain the lower unemployment rate -- those gaining advanced work qualification would not be seeking menial employment to fund their education, nor would they be going into debt to acquire the skills which would later enhance their nations GDP.

Regan was complaining that students were treated like they belonged to the Tribe of Issachar – scholars to be prized. Jesus was a scholar, the son of a carpenter who could afford to teach because Hebrew culture supported him. In Denmark, hard work, talent, and motivation determine your ability to get an education, not your parents wealth, or your willingness to accrue a lifetime debt in the form of student loans.

The World Economic Forum ranking of the best-educated populations Denmark was somewhat better than the USA, and when it comes to the human capital index, the USA was 4th and Denmark 5th – Norway, Finland, and Switzerland, in that order, comprised the top three. It's worth noting that, in January 2018, around the time the rankings were published showing Norway first among nations, Trump made his infamous remark about not wanting people from "shithole countries, ... *we should have more people from Norway.*"

Naturally, the haters denounced Trump as a racist because he acknowledged being aware of World Economic Forum facts, and wanted immigrants from "the best-educated" nations, rather than the functional illiterates his critics seem to prefer. Note, the most educated are people in nations where socialism dates back a thousand years – to the time of the Vikings.

The anti-Trump media missed the reality of what he was saying – #MAGA means being better than number one, it does not have a structure. It involves attracting those who are #one and so, once again, America becomes the "Land of Opportunity."

There is no conflict between opportunity and tighter border control, but there is hypocrisy associated with Schumer, who now opposes the steel fence wall when, in 2013, he pushed Senate legislation to add 700-miles of Border Fence/Wall to the 650 miles constructed by Obama as the first phase of the 2006 Secure Fence Act. It also exposes hypocrisy on the part of Obama, when he gives speeches about the poor migrants.

On 3 March 2019, the Associated Press {AP} reported on the "Border agents using firearms less" – less than they did under Obama, specifically: *"There were 15 instances where officers and agents used firearms during the budget year 2018, down from a high of 55 was reported during the 2012 budget year, and down from 17 during 2017's budget year and 25 the budget year before."*

This means that, compared to Obama in 2012, agents under Trump used 73% less lethal force on those "poor migrants." The AP also reported that the use of less-lethal force is also down. It might be worth noting that, in January and February 2019, nearly 100,000 families were apprehended attempting illegal entry via locations between ports of entry. Were this pattern to continue, it could mean over 1.2 million apprehensions for 2019, with the possibility that the number would exceed the 1.6 million attained in 2000.

In terms of the Welfare system that Conservatives label as Socialism – either the United States or Mexico provide support for these people. Mexico, because, while the California Court has declared, when apprehended, illegals have the legal right to claim asylum, the Trump Administration has initiated a policy where asylum seekers are returned to Mexico while their cases await adjudication. This would shift a long-term support burden from

American border communities and onto Mexico. Whether or not the Wall is built, Mexico is going to pay for the migrants it allows to enter its Southern Border.

Turning our attention back to Norway and the invitation inferred by Trump's comment, history tells us that, between 1870 to 1910 the United States welcomed nearly a quarter of Norway's working-age population; while there were negatives associated with that period – it was still one of the high-points in American growth and expansion.

As covered in the 2017 book, "Jonathon's POTUS Cousins," the American "Progressive" movement can be traced to Marxist related Socialist ideas of equality and freedom which gave rise to the Forty-Eighter (1848) Movement that swept Europe before it failed, and many of its adherents migrated to America, eventually settling in the Midwest – which gave rise to the politics of Lincoln.

The American "melting pot" served as a laboratory for the formulation of ideas about rights, innate abilities, and race. Those ideas, combined with the antisemitism which was defined by the Inquisition and adopted by the German Lutheran religion, served as a basis for formulating theories of eugenics and race superiority which were the basis for doctrines espoused by Adolph Hitler and his Nazis followers.

In terms of this book series, and the related examinations into historic dating and "prophecy," the United States has shared a symbiotic connection to Germany, which has manifested in the Progressive Movement.

We can play with the dates, but Socialism in America can be assigned to the people variously known as Amish, Mennonite, or Pennsylvania Dutch, who are associated with "Barn Raising"– the practice of the community uniting to provide free labor for the construction of a barn or house for a community member. This is one of many such practices predating the American Revolution, and, we could assert, predates Karl Marx by a century. Thus we can assert that when Philadelphia became one of the cradles of Liberty American the soon to be new nation already had a strong Socialist footing supporting its Foundation.

Between April and August 1844, Marx, a Jew, wrote a series of Economic and Philosophic Manuscripts expanding upon the dictum of Hegelian philosophy which holds that "*the rational alone is real,*" or that which is real can be categorized in a way which allows it to be expressed rationally.

This same approach also generates the dialectic debate typical of scientific thought and theory, unless it involves the assertion of unfounded supposition, approximate or half-truths, stubborn skepticism, or outright lies. In the latter context, we see an appearance of this complete ignorance and intellectual poverty that marks attacks on Socialism and also on many aspects of the Trump Administration.

Socialism is necessary to protect the average person. When we view the battle between capitalists and workers, between the 1% and everyone else, the capitalist must always win, because they have the resources to outlive the workers.

But, as we learned from both Barnum and the Bible, when reality sets in, the capitalist relies upon and must yield to those who are educated and have good health. So it is that, when they are fighting the masses, the capitalist will attack both education and healthcare. When the masses wish to enjoy prosperity, their leaders will promote the Socialist agenda based upon both free education and universal healthcare.

In 1935, President Franklin D. Roosevelt signed the Social Security Act into law; on 22 June 1944, Roosevelt signed the GI Bill, which provided education benefits – access to colleges and universities – which would eventually benefit 8 million veterans and provide a foundation for the economic growth which defined the childhood of the Baby-Boom generation.

As part of the GI Bill signing, the Roosevelt progressive agenda also included the Servicemen's Readjustment Act of 1944, which, by 1955, provided about $33 billion to cover 4.3 million home loans. This was the monetary equivalent of a Socialist or Amish "Barn Raising"; and, when combined with higher incomes earned by those who took advantage of the educational benefits, the enhanced tax revenues at all levels of government meant the GI Bill paid for itself many times over.

Socialist programs, in the capitalist context education and property ownership, tend to finance themselves. The same thing can be said for above poverty Minimum Wages and Social Security

– *"Old-Age, Survivors, and Disability Insurance"* – benefits.

If someone actually accepted the Old Testament, or New Testament teachings assigned to Jesus, they would understand that they both mandate above poverty Social Security; if they also understood economics, they would know reducing or eliminating poverty enhances and strengthens an economy.

For the slave master who claims to be a capitalist, the true lesson is lost. Similarly, this is a lesson lost on the Evangelical Conservatives who oppose anything labeled Socialist.

All economies are based on the disposable income of the poorest member of society. Capitalists need people to buy their goods and services. In an agrarian society, the master can afford slaves – until the culture raises to the level of requiring "luxury goods" which must be traded for or purchased. When the culture is primitive, all the goods needed can be harvested or constructed from available resources. Modern societies involve the purchase of raw materials and conversion those materials into marketable products.

In the 2011 book, "Grandpa was a Deity," we learned that all modern civilizations evolved from one migratory population which specialized in knowledge transfer and used as its authority the idea they were the "children of the sons of the creator Deity." Their commodity was "divine authority" derived from education and knowledge. This allowed them to acquire "wealth" and make it immune to detrimental human activities.

Granted, there are people who are poor out of choice, or because they want to live off others – this choice can be based on service to others, as in Matthew 19:21, *"If you want to be perfect, go, sell your possessions and give to the poor, and you will have treasure in heaven. Then come, follow me."*

The scriptures say the believers they visit will provide food and lodging – making it a Socialist religion, and means those who oppose Socialism opposes Jesus. We know they do not hesitate to invoke Biblical authority to justify oppressing others.

The bottom line is, the ideas behind Socialist philosophy are as old as civilization and augment Capitalist prosperity – or there would be no logic to having the Biblical Merchant Tribe fund and fully support the Tribe of Scholars.

CHAPTER FOUR – DEPRESSION
**"Happiness is not in the mere possession of money.
It lies in the joy of achievement and in the thrill of
creative effort."**
~ Franklin Delano Roosevelt

The day after editing the previous chapter, A story showed up in my email which, ostensibly, dealt with the manner in which Torah – the Old Testament – teaches about the need for financial transparency. But, it also teaches about Biblical Socialism in its purest form. Now we need to recognize that, at the very mention of religion, many will roll their eyes and turn away.

It is rather humorous to note that both the Bible and Koran cite this era as the one when traditional religion with its pagan practices or rites will come to an end – and we need only be aware of world events to bear witness to the accuracy of that prediction.

Consistent with ancient practice, in Exodus 25 we see that, when Moses lead the people out of Israel, it became necessary to give them a focal point for their newly emerging religion – this was a portable structure known as the tabernacle, a word which means *"dwelling place."* And here we are told, after affirming the traditional practice of giving offerings, supposedly, the Lord tells Moses he shall *"Then have them make a sanctuary for me, and I will dwell among them."*

The chapter then describes the design of the structure and the wooden ark which is the container for the covenant law – the Ten Commandments. In "GENESIS OF GENESIS", the 2012 book which explains the math of Genesis the underlays the patriarch ages, we see how the writers of the Old Testament used existing mythology and custom to ensure a familiarity upon which to base their new and evolved religion. Having a tabernacle, and later a Temple or Church, provided a community center where people would gather and organize the socialist activities which were *"an atonement"* – a way of giving back to the community.

In Exodus 25:11, we see the atonement also has an element of taxation accompanied by a serious penalty: *"When you take a census of the Israelites to count them, each one must pay the*

Lord a ransom for his life at the time he is counted. Then no

plague will come on them when you number them." This tax is paid by everyone over the age of twenty who wants to be counted as part of the community. And, as with most of the Bible, there are health-code aspects: *"they shall wash with water so that they will not die."* Knowing of diseases, bacteria and the basis for the rules of modern hygiene, is there a necessity to explain this? And then, we also have the establishment of a standard work week, *"For six days work is to be done, but the seventh day is a day of Sabbath rest,"* which ensures people don't work themselves to death.

We can jump ahead to Exodus 36:5 and see the tabernacle was a "barn raising" – skilled workers donating their time and using materials freely donated. In fact, more was donated than was needed, so we are told, *"The people are bringing more than enough for doing the work the Lord commanded to be done."*

Freewill offerings morning after morning. So all the skilled workers who were doing all the work on the Sanctuary left what they were doing and said to Moses, *"The people are bringing more than enough for doing the work the Lord commanded to be done."* As a result, Moses orders that *"No man or woman is to make anything else as an offering for the sanctuary. And so the people were restrained from bringing more because what they already had was more than enough to do all the work."*

This is the crux of the truest form oh socialist behavior, a nation where people need not be asked to give more, but are told they have given too much. They do not stop, instead, they redirect their efforts to charitable giving, *"tzedakah"* where people do not behave with the attitude *"Oh, if only I could do that, be like that,"* but instead they take a positive approach by asserting, *"If they can do that, then...I can too."*

Most people know the golden rule, but few of them act on it from the Talmudic Socialist perspective that holds: *"Whatever I want for myself, I want the same for that other person."*

Or, as expressed by Maimonides, *"And whatever I do not want for myself or my friends, I do not want for that other person. This is the meaning of the verse, 'And you shall love the other person as yourself.'"* (Leviticus 19:18)

Look at the phrasing used by President Trump. When he spoke of health care, he looked at Australia and said we should have the same or better; when he spoke of immigration, he looked to Norway and its highly educated population. But, even as he said he wanted that caliber of person – the level America is going to fill the jobs that will, in the decade to come, be unfilled for lack of people, lack of population – he also said he wanted lawfully admitted immigrants from Latin America.

Note that people attack Trump for his words and phrasing, but they make it a point to avoid his actual actions as President. As we are told in Pirke Avot 1:17, *"Shimon [the son of Rabban Gamliel] says: It is not what one says, but rather what one does, that makes all the difference in the world."* For those who are not aware, *Rabban Gamliel* was a contemporary of Jesus, Peter, and Paul, who taught basically the same lessons Jesus had sought to teach; in this instance, his words are basically Matthew 7:16.

POTUS Cousin Winston Churchill once said, *"We make a living by what we get, but we make a life by what we give."*

Another POTUS Cousin, Theodore Roosevelt, said: *"It is not the critic who counts, or how the strong man stumbled and fell, or where the doer of deeds could have done better. The credit belongs to the man who is actually in the arena, whose face is marred by dust and sweat and blood, who strives valiantly, who errs and comes up short again and again, who knows the great enthusiasm, the great devotion, and spends himself in a worthy cause; and if he fails, at least fails while daring greatly, so that he will never be with those cold and timid souls who know neither victory nor defeat."*

If we think of those words, can any honest person not do so without associating them with Donald Trump and his effort to formally bring an end to the Korean War, or seek to restore the outsourced industries America has lost during the sixty-five years since the Armistice ended the military aspect of that conflict?

In his *"Laws of Gifts to the poor, 10:1-3"*, Maimonides said of the Jewish spirit (hence of Jesus and all who claim to follow Him), *"If someone is cruel and does not show mercy, there are sufficient grounds to suspect his lineage, since cruelty is found only among the other nations."* So we need to look at the impact of actions and political positions because we are looking at the National attitude and not just that of the individual.

Is there cruelty in constructing a Border Wall so as to direct people to a port of entry where they can be admitted in an orderly manner? Or does the cruelty stem from having them enter with no documentation or legal means of support while making it a crime for employers to hire them without that documentation?

Clearly, if they cannot legally work, they will need charity to support them, and such charity will become a burden on the communities where the undocumented settle – while draining the resources needed for legal residents. As Maimonides went on to say, "*Whoever refuses to give charity is called Belial, the same term which is applied to idol worshipers.*" Which means that those who would deny Food Stamps (SNAP), low-income heating (LIHEAP), or any level of decent housing to the illegals is little more than an idol worshiper – a reality Republican Conservatives and their Evangelical bass would do well to remember when they attack Welfare, raising the minimum wage, or failing to lift the contribution and benefit levels on Social Security.

There is an economic crash or dramatic transition due; the book "*A Brewing Storm: How Trump helped delay an impending doom,*" published in June 2018, examined the Great Depression and the current developing economic situation. Five years prior to the Depression, Nikolai Kondratiev published his first book on major economic cycle theory which would become known as the Kondratiev Wave or K-WAVE. Based on the K-WAVE cycles, the year 2027 should see an economic crash in what now constitutes the European Union.

There is no question or rational basis to dispute observed economic cycles or wave patterns. Of course, people can argue the "exact date" – but who cares if it is 2027 or 2025 or 2029? As was presented in the 2014 book, on dating the Revelation prophecies, "*Biblical Prophecy: Are we in the Revelation Era,*" there is a combination of starting dates and calendars used can introduce a variation of plus-or-minus two years.

In the book, as in the title system used in this series on the Trump Era, and in the K-WAVE, there is a consistent generational element of 56-60 years. This is consistent with the concept behind

Exodus 20:5, "*punishing the children for the sin of the parents to the third and fourth generation.*" Consistent with the idea that an invisible deity will inflict the punishment – which is the idea that "Lady Luck" turns against us, or whatever third party we seek to blame for events in our lives – the underlying observation is that the logic behind our actions and the decisions we make will be taught to out children and then they will teach it to their children.

If that logic is flawed or involves something inherently harmful, then the real damage or harm often appears in the third generation. If your grandparents smoked, your parents probably did, and that means your generation was probably exposed to two generations of secondhand smoke.

Is this relevant to anything we are looking at? What could smoking have to do with anything political or economic?

The answer is in the medical journals and generally ignored as secondary to such things like the risk for heart, vascular, and lung disease. Few people are aware that, by the third generation, smoking can cause fertility problems for both genders – minor stuff like erectile dysfunction and pregnancy complication rates are increased by smoking. After three or four generations of the Tobacco Industry pushing cigarettes, nations where cigarettes or cigars are mid-twentieth century symbols, are now showing the lowest fertility rates. A curious coincidence.

Right now, America enjoys a knee-jerk reaction to calling someone a Socialist. In the 1800s it was simply being Progressive – but then it became associated with Communism, and, after the Second World War, being a Communist became "bad" and a target for McCarthyism; it also worked to mask being an anti-Semite; as we saw, Socialism is Talmudic, Marx was a Jew, if you want to be an anti-Semite, but don't want it known, simply attack Socialism – makes it easy to attack Bernie Sanders.

If we listen to the rhetoric, rather than simply echoing it, it becomes apparent that there is a sense of emotional depression sweeping across the nation. It actually has nothing to do with the "State of the Nation," and far more to do with the average age of the population and, by extension, the average age of Congress – which, in 2019, was sixty and its leadership is over seventy, and the average America thirty-eight. In terms of age, America ranks

61st in the world; the European Union and the other European States are older, while China is slightly younger, and the Islamic nations average a decade younger.

Gerontocracy – government ruled by old people – creates a subliminal emotion fear of a break in political continuity that will bring about the fall of the nation. That fall comes because the continuity assumed when making long-term plans is shattered.

If someone needs a reason to be depressed, its because the average national age means the Islamic nations have more people of military age, and, in a decade, will have even more. As those who saw the *Revelation* timeline in *"Biblical Prophecy"* know, the period 2033/35 is of the Koran's Islamic Jihad that kills the "evil Christians" – the world can either call it the Apocalypse or simply World War Three. To wage that war, Iran and/or the Saudis will need nuclear weapons.

Then we have the economic depression which must serve as a prelude to the war – the same as the Great Depression set the stage for the Second World War. Events in 2019 are beginning to look a lot like those that created World War One – at least when Trump is attacked for sidestepping the killing of Saudi opposition author Jamal Ahmad Khashoggi.

Think in terms of the assassination of Archduke Ferdinand – a minor nobleman of no world significance, beyond the idea that his death would serve as the excuse to trigger the start of World War One. A few people in media seem to be upset that Trump is not escalating matters over the death of an insignificant writer or that of Otto Frederick Warmbier – a college student, arrested and imprisoned for theft, who died soon after being released from a North Korean prison.

Looking for other parallels, the pre-Great War period was one of high immigration and migration, which also gave rise to a rabble-rousing Hearst Publications spawned tabloid media which promoted what became the Spanish American War concurrent with Germany building up its maritime forces after France and Russia signed an agreement which sparked fear and resentment in Berlin. Then, within two years, the world began a new century of social and economic change which sparked Nationalist waves of the type now defining European and American politics.

Today, the message being transmitted on "social media" is to antagonize any and all potential enemies with an eye toward obstructing negotiations nations that are in a position to disrupt global stability. Variations on this are playing out across Europe.

The pattern echoes that leading to The Great War. We are seeing a growth of nationalism, a focus on wealth which is now term Oligarchs, the economic rivalry has shifted with America going overboard on devoting money to its military at the cost to the welfare of the population, and, where there Spanish American War played against the background of Britain in China, we now have America playing off China against a backdrop of the Middle Eastern conflict initiated by when the Bush Presidents decided to attack and kill Saddam Hussein but allowed Osama bin Laden to walk. Then, on 2 May 2011, under Obama, things changed when U.S. Special Forces raided an al Qaeda compound in Abbottabad, Pakistan, and killed Osama.

Fortunately, very few people believe in patterns of human behavior – some subliminal needs to repeat the past in a modern context. Yet it is one of the forces that might underlie the idea that the sins and iniquities of one generation are passed down to subsequent ones. Each generation paraphrases the behavior of its parents. The changes can be attributed to the influence of friends and the surrounding culture. In the modern world, cross-cultural influences are imposed and amplified by social and entertainment media to influence and quickly define popular culture.

One observed pattern is that of OMER, an ancient unit of measure equal to seven-times-seven. Some people might recall the Aladdin line about being the seventh son of a seventh son and the mystical power comes with seventh son status. There is also the 56-57 year astronomical cycle built into Stonehenge, which is three of the nineteen-year Metonic cycles which form the basis of the Hebrew and ancient Chinese Calendars.

Those familiar with the book "Genesis of Genesis" already know the Patriarch ages are functions of 19 linked the start other ancient calendars by periods divisible to 19. They also know that the modern western calendar is Hebrew Calendar reset to one at the 198th Metonic node.

In the context of repeating history, coincidence can be very weird – the time lapse between the killing of Ferdinand and Bin Laden is 96 years, which is a period equal to the sum of 49 and 57.

These cycles come into play when placed in the context of BREXIT and the economic difficulties evidenced in France, Spain, Italy, and Greece. Back in the 1920s, Russian economist Nikolai Kondratiev observed a cyclical pattern that reflected an apparent 49 to 57-year cycle in data extending back to 10th-century China. His observation, now known as the K-WAVE, predicts a serious recession or depression roughly every fifty-seven years.

After the 1929 Great Depression imposed itself on Europe and America, Kondratiev made the mistake of telling Stalin the capitalist system would not collapse, it would adjust. Stalin was intrigued; when Kondratiev proved correct, Stalin ordered Nikolai executed and, for two decades, did Stalin did his best to suppress the economic findings – during which time the theories of British economist John Maynard Keynes came into prominence.

The key idea is that there are cycles. There is no obvious logic to explain them, but they are there and they hold over time.

In terms of 57, that's Stonehenge; it's three Metonic cycles in both the Chinese and Hebrew; in terms of America, can look at George Washington's inauguration on 30 April 1789, count 57 four-year election cycles (228 years) to arrive at 20 January 2017 and the inauguration of Donald John Trump. Those who familiar with Stonehenge know it has 56 upright stones, and transferred to the Presidential Election cycle means the Obama's Second term – the period when Trump was elected – was the transitional period beginning the next cycle.

Those who read *"Genesis of Genesis"* already know about the 224 year cycle – the Flood Story which, through the *"Shem Error,"* provided the means by which the authors corrected for the three-years lost over the three cycles between the birth of Enoch and that of Arpachshad (the first born after the mythical Flood).

As a period of transition, we can expect major changes and revelations. We have the Mueller Investigation and its successful indictments and convictions; in March 2019, the media reported: *"Major Democratic and Republican donors were indicted Tuesday in a college admissions scandal that also led to the arrests of Wall Street CEOs, famous actresses, and Silicon Valley executives."*

For the past century, various factions have been calling for people to *"Drain the {political and capitalist} Swamp."* As with MAGA, Ronald Reagan used the slogan in his campaign and early in his administration. As a political metaphor, it is ideally applied to Washington – which was constructed on a drained swamp.

In 1903, Winfield Romeo Gaylord wrote, "*Socialists are not satisfied with killing a few of the mosquitoes which come from the capitalist swamp. They want to drain the swamp.*" What is curious is that, as a member of the Socialist Party of America, he was stating his party's goals, which, eighty years later, became the exact same goals of the Conservative Republican, anti-Socialist, Ronald Wilson Reagan; then became center stage among Reagan-Democrats.

Later, in as the 2000 Reform Party presidential candidate, Pat Buchanan declared: *"Neither Beltway party is going to drain this swamp: it's a protected wetland; they breed in it, they spawn in it."*

On 14 December 2006, Nancy Patricia Pelosi would claim, *"I honestly believe you cannot advance the people's agenda unless you drain the swamp that is Washington D.C.."* A month earlier, Pelosi had defined the term: *"'Drain the swamp' means to turn this Congress into the most honest and open Congress in history. That's my pledge — that is what I intend to do."*

There is an old idiom, *"when you are up to your neck in alligators, it is hard to remember your objective was to drain the swamp'."* But, when *"The Swamp Fights Back,"* that's exactly where you will be, it is where Trump has been since he won the Electoral College vote and thus the election. The problem being, some of those alligators are the international or global economic cycles which are associated with various forms of Nationalism we see sweeping across Europe in the form of BREXIT and the Yellow Vest Movement.

What Kondratiev had realized was something similar to the dating system which was the basis for the events in *The Book of Revelation* – events follow a pattern related to the generations that experience them. In terms of the international mercantile credit system or Revelation forecast, basic human behavior serves to connect events over a period of either 49 or 57 years – the time in which we can produce three to four generations, which is easily encompassed within sixty years.

It is not 'exact,' because reproductive rates are not precise and, therefore, the generational transfer varies. Yet it can still be averaged out to maintain the predictive nature of events. In the case of the K-WAVE, it would appear that the next Depression is on track for the year 2027, and BREXIT is serving as the catalyst.

In the United States, the Obama Recovery, which Trump has worked to continue, is a direct result of an aging Baby-Boomer population combined with Negative Population Growth. Granted, American NPG has yet to reach levels that define the Developed World, but then, America has historically lagged behind patterns of social evolutionary change. But that does not mean it fails to adhere to the cyclical patterns.

Looking at both the K-WAVE and the critical periods that defined post-Revolutionary American history, we acknowledged that the Stonehenge cycles of 56 and 57 coincide the period that defines the second term of the Obama Administration.

If we apply the 49-cycle OMER to the four-year presidential election cycle, we see it coincides with the nation's 196th year, 1985, the start of the second term of the Reagan Administration and the affirmation of an era when deficits and runaway National Debt would define the American economy and set-it-up for a new Great Depression.

In 1975, while visiting the Johnny Carson Show, Reagan said, "*When they give me a choice between a $53 billion deficit in the budget and an $80 deficit, when budget deficits are what's causing inflation, I don't see that there's any room to be on either side of that argument.*"

Then, when Carson asked him, "*How do you balance the budget?*" Reagan simply replied: "*It's like protecting your virtue. You have to learn to say no.*"

Of course, Reagan was basically criticizing Jimmy Carter in much the same way as Donald Trump criticized Barack Obama for playing golf. And his "*learn to say no*" would later become Nancy Reagan's "*Just Say No*" campaign against drugs in the form of crack cocaine, which, thirst years later, was replaced by Fentanyl addiction.

But, as Reagan demonstrated when you are in the Oval, perspective changes. So it was that, from 1974 and throughout Reagan's Administration, Federal Deficits grew at historical rates, then settled in before the 1988 election, only to result in the climb through the Bush-41 Administration.

With the 1992 election of Clinton, the period from 20 January 1993 to 20 January 2001 became one defined by shrinking deficits that soon became budgetary surpluses. The Republican response came on 19 December 1998, when they impeached Clinton for Oral in the Oval.

With Bush-43 came the steepest rise in deficits since the 1960s, which culminated in the Great Recession of 2007/8 which caused the 2009 deficit to approach $1.55 Trillion; since then it has steadily fallen, reaching a low of $395 Billion in 2018. There is a curious fact, in the post-war period leading up to *The Great Depression*, there was a steady Federal Budget surplus.

While the numbers tell us nothing about the cycles; when examined a fiscal year basis, they indicate the cumulative growth of the National Debt and that it can be directly connected to the fiscal irresponsibility of Conservative Republicans.

If we use the Great Depression as year-zero, going back 56-57 years brings us to The Long Depression of 1873; going forward we would expect a significant economic problem in 1986 only to discover Black Monday, 19 October 1987 – which parallels Black Monday and Black Tuesday on 28 and 29 October 1929. If the pattern holds, we should have until 2044 before we see the next Black Monday.

If we use OMER, 49-years prior to 1929 is 1880 and we get nothing; 49-years after, yields 1978, which misses the OPEC oil embargo by five years, but yields the reason Jimmy Carter lost his re-election bid, then, from July 1981 to November 1982 provided Reagan with a recession to define his first year in office. And, even though he produced Budget surpluses, from July 1990 to March 1991, Clinton had to deal with the 1989 savings and loan crisis – which sparked a 3.9% drop in GDP and 7.8% unemployment.

Of course, Bush-43 was welcomed into office by the Dot-com crash of March to November 2001, and then it was topped off by the 9/11 high point destruction of the World Trade Center. In return, Bush gifted America with the longest undeclared war in the Nation's history, and Obama with the Great Recession.

Everyone has a recession. If you followed the news media in 2018, Trump should already have one of his own; even if you didn't, there seems to be a recession every 6-10 years, which means there should have been one before October 2018. And that explains why the financial-types spent Trumps second 56-weeks predicting one.

If Trump's such an incompetent idiot, what went wrong? Why is unemployment at a record low? Why are wages growing? Why is the economy growing at a record pace? What went wrong with the traditional economic pattern?

Is it possible Trump has scared the Swamp Denizens into submission – or maybe they are regrouping for the same tactical change they have wanted since the 2016 election?

CHAPTER FIVE – HARM OTHERS

"The oleaginous Mike Pence,
with his talent for toadyism
and appetite for obsequiousness,..."
~ George F. Will, Washington Post 9 May 2018

From the moment the Electoral Vote results were determined, there has been a movement to Impeach Trump and elevate Mike Pence to the Oval Office. But the conversation was reported on 17 April 2016, when Darren Samuelsohn, a senior policy reporter for *Politico*, wrote: *"'Impeachment' is already on the lips of pundits, newspaper editorials, constitutional scholars, and even a few members of Congress."*

Samuelsohn then noted: *"It's not unusual for controversial presidents to be shadowed by talk of impeachment, once they've been in office long enough to make people mad. But before he's elected? Before he's a nominee?"*

The propaganda machine was echoing the *"Lock Her Up"* slogan, prior to Trumps nomination. They were, in effect, rigging the election by sabotaging a potential candidate with the threat that he would be impeached upon being sworn in.

What rational entity would threaten a course of conduct, so disruptive that, when used against Nixon, the Stock Market lost 45% of its value, and every foreign policy initiative came to a halt?

Consider the level negative sentiment and pure political manipulation that would be necessary to invent the grounds for a valid and historically significant impeachment – one that would end with a Senate conviction of High Crimes and Misdemeanors so egregious and yet without compelling evidence which could be used during the course of the election to prevent Trump for even being elected.

A week after the election, on 14 November 2016, T.A. Frank wrote in Vanity Fair "WILL TRUMP BE IMPEACHED?" The article began with, *"Do a LexisNexis search, and you'll find that "Trump" and some variant of "impeach" have already appeared in 37 newspaper headlines."* Frank went on to remind readers that only Andrew Jackson and Bill Clinton had actually undergone the experience, and that: "*Legally, impeachment, which is like an indictment, requires serious wrongdoing in order to be invoked —'Treason, Bribery, or other High Crimes and Misdemeanors,' according to the Constitution.*"

What's never mentioned is that Jackson was the only President to actually pay-off the National Debt and still produce a Budget Surplus, and Clinton turned two decades of record Deficits into a record budget Surplus. Trump? The self-promoter behind "*The Art of the Deal.*" He was clearly a threat to all who want the National Debt to grow to the point where the nation could no longer meet both its debt service and obligations to its citizens.

Obama had nothing he could be attacked for – other than being the son of a Kenyan. It is Politically Incorrect to yell race, so we heard claims he was really born in Kenya and the Hawaiian Health Department mention of his birth in their routine statical Births-Deaths-Marriages report to the media was a lie. It would not generate impeachment, rather it would remove him as Constitutionally ineligible – never mind the fact they also declared the Canadian born Ted Cruz a "Natural Born Citizen," after all, he was white, with a Cuban Communist father.

In all four instances we are exposed to varying levels of power politics but those who profit from government money and deficits. Of note is their ability to distract the public from thinking in terms of real issues. In that regard, their success can be seen in a February Opinion Poll in which our "mystical" 56 appears as 56 percent of registered Democrats saying, regardless of a candidates position on issues important to them, their top priority was that the candidate could beat Trump.

This supports or explains the drive for impeachment that would install a theocratic conservative who, in only three years as governor of Indiana, demonstrated an ability to inflict economic and social harm upon his state.

At the same time, A Pew Research Center poll in January found that 53 percent of Democrats wanted the party to become more moderate, while only 40 percent wanted it to become more liberal. So we have some evidence that Democratic voters are in the process of following Pelosi and Schumer to become Reagan-

Democrats. They are moving to the Right and they do not care about the policies of the candidates who lead them there. When viewed in a context of the ease with which Bernie Sanders seems to be racking in campaign contributions and in the numbers who flocked an 8 March 2019 rally at the University of Iowa. Clearly, Sanders is about as liberal as one can get – he checks all the boxes as a Jewish Progressive Liberal Socialist. Moreover, we have the popularity of the nation's youngest Congresswoman, Alexandra Ocasio-Cortez [AOC], who is right there next to Bernie.

Supposedly, people join campaigns because the issues are something they deeply care about, and they want a candidate who focuses on those issues. These issues of importance and meaning bring the transformative excitement that translates into victory.

Since Bernie is not a POTUS Cousin, if he is nominated, he has no chance of winning. However, former Colorado Gov. John Hickenlooper is a POTUS Cousin, as are Elizabeth Warren and Joe Bidden. The fact that Mike Pence is not part of the historic family provides a shield against Trump's Impeachment.

Even when Nixon clearly was in line to make history, as the first President convicted by the Senate, Spiro Agnew had to be removed so that a Cousin, Gerald Ford, could assume the Oval Office. Once Ford had been installed, the Republicans were free to turn on their own and let Nixon know he could either resign or be convicted – which, then would mean criminal prosecution.

In the second week of March 2019, former Vice President Joe Biden decided to criticize Trump's 2020 budget proposal by declaring, *"Did you see the budget that was just introduced? Almost a trillion dollar cut in Medicare. ...Why? Because of a tax cut for the super wealthy that created a deficit of $1.9 trillion, and now they gotta go make somebody pay for it."*

Of course, in the age of the fact-check, we can check Biden's numbers and discover the Federal Budget Deficit for FY2019 is projected to be 980 billion, and for 2020. $1.1 trillion – Biden lied and simply doubled the projected 2019 numbers.

He could prove correct, but only if the economy tanks and revenues fall – something that is easily achieved by flooding the nation with unprocessed asylum seekers. Such an influx, most of whom being children and unable to support themselves, could cost the various local governments in excess of $1000 each per month, or $12,000/year. The March 2019 Border Patrol estimate was that there would be over a million such individuals, meaning a drain on the economy of about $12 Billion for the year – unless Trump sends the applicants back to Mexico while their cases are processed – the economic multiplier turns that cost into a GDP loss of over $700 Billion and provides the basis for Biden's claim.

The costs come from the fact that the asylum seekers are mostly children, were they adult it would be different – at least according to the Pew Research Center which, on 7 March 2019, published an article entitled *"Latinos' Incomes Higher Than Before Great Recession, but U.S.-Born Latinos Yet to Recover."*

It turns out that, for all of the economic recovery gains made since Bush's attempt to destroy the economy, and the wage income growth, between 2007 and 2017, Latinos have seen their median income increase by 5%. This figure hides the fact that, in 2017, incomes for U.S.-born Latinos were 6% BELOW their 2007 levels, while their foreign-born kinsmen had incomes that were 14% higher than their 2007 levels.

The report tells us that *"Longer-tenured immigrants earn more than the typical immigrant, and their rising share gave a sizable boost to the average income of foreign-born Latinos."* A fact that reflects well on the economic reasons *'Dreamers'* should be legally integrated into the American culture.

As for the cuts to Medicare, these appear to be related to the budget proposals to cut the cost of the covered medications. If the Congress drafted and adopted laws that could achieve the stated goals, the cuts are more than paid for.

As the proposed Budget Stated: *"The Budget also prevents manufacturers from using authorized generics to lower their rebate obligations, and includes payment changes so State Medicaid programs do not overpay for generic drugs, saving money for States and taxpayers."* If this could be achieved, States would benefit and be able to expand coverage, with a detrimental effect on their budgets.

Of course, as we know from his time in Indiana, a President Pence would bring about a cost increase, by doing away with key programs.

While Biden, like the rest of those who would rather bring down then create, loves to attack without improvement. Implicit in his comment on Trump's Budget, is that he would retain, and maybe expand, the deficits by that *"trillion dollar"* figure – or, he could seek to rescind the Tax Reform legislation.

Of course, if he were to adopt the Bernie Sander Social Security related proposal and remove the cap on income subject to contributions, sufficient funds would be generated to expand Medicare coverage or create the Medicare-for-all program for any and all legal citizens. As an added benefit, those portions of the National Debt held by foreign nations could be repatriated and the risks of default are eliminated.

(For those who do not grasp how the Negative Population Growth combined with a Baby Boom population already on Social Security, affects the National Debt: the Social Security funds are Treasury notes and part of the National Debt; by 2055 the Baby-boomers will all be either deceased or setting Guinness World Records for longevity. NPG means nobody is replacing them and therefore there will be nobody to claim the money representing the "Trust Account" portion of the National Debt. Between that, and inflation devaluing the debt, most of the Debt is nullified and can be written off.)

In a statement relevant to Biden's, the Acting Office of Management and Budget {OMB} Director, Russ Vought, stated *"What we are doing is putting forward reforms that lower drug prices, that because Medicare pays a very large share of drug prices in this country, it has the impact of finding savings. We're also finding waste, fraud, and abuse. But Medicare spending will go up every single year by healthy margins, and there are no structural changes for Medicare beneficiaries."* Thus, Vought established the Budget cut reflected projected saving, while actual benefits would rise.

Again, fact-checking, we find, in August 2012 the Obama-Biden administration proposed cutting $716 billion from Medicare programs. Trump's proposed cut was $845 billion – not *"Almost a trillion"*– a rhetorical difference which has significance when we consider the Obama-Biden cuts, eight years earlier, would be $787 billion if expressed in 2019 dollars. A $59 Billion dollar difference in "real dollars."

Now, if we look at those covered, in 2012 the combined Medicare and Medicare Advantage programs covered 48,722,929 individuals; in 2018 that number had climbed to 59,869,402; so, in 2019 dollars, the per capita cut sought by Obama was $16,152, while the Trump cut would be $14,114. That is, when viewed on a per capita basis, adjusted for inflation, Obama's cuts were 14% higher than those proposed by Trump.

In the context of Medicare, Medicare, and the Right-wing attacks on Obamacare, it is worth looking at the legislative record of both Mike Pence – the man who would be President if Trump was impeached – and Senate Minority Leader Chuck Schumer.

Pence propensities are routinely called out. As Governor of Indiana, he oversaw enactment of Conservative values. It took less than three years for him to enacted conservative health care reforms, tightened abortion restrictions and slashed taxes.

On 26 March 2015, Pence signed Indiana Senate Bill 101, into law. Entitled the Religious Freedom Restoration Act (RFRA), it created the right of individuals and companies to argue that a law or practice would somehow impede their exercise of religion or substantially burden its practice.

The Indiana law was a variation on legislation introduced by Senator Chuck Schumer and signed into law by Bill Clinton on 16 November 1993 – in 1997, its provisions regarding states rights were determined to be unconstitutional.

For individuals, the Schumer and Pence legislation opened the door to the March 2019 lawsuit by Kentucky high school student who, among others, was subject of the Northern Kentucky Health Department imposed a three-week ban for unvaccinated students to attend classes after an outbreak of chickenpox. Basically, the student is asserting a religious right to become a potential "Typhoid Mary."

Schumer, Pence, and others across the nation are attacking the national healthcare system by establishing laws which allow the assertion of medieval superstition and misrepresentation of scripture to endanger the health, wellbeing and the lives others as part of their political agenda.

As was established in the Hobby-Lobby case, the laws were designed to grant privately held Corporations the right to demonstrate and exercise bigotry by an assertion of a religion that neither it nor its owners adhere to – it's a variant on *"Saint Paul's Joke"*, the book which the Vatican studied before Pope Benedict took the historically significant action of retiring.

As with Schumer's Religious Freedom Act, the Indiana law has the effect of legalizing discrimination against LGBT people based on an alleged anti-homosexuality verse which applies only to bisexual males – as anyone who has read the bible, or *"Saint Paul's Joke"*, is aware, no similar verse exists for women, and the only women subject to punishment are those who knowingly help males to violate Leviticus 18:22, *"A man shall not lie with a male as with a woman; it is an abomination."*

It's interesting that Pence signed a law based on adherence to religion, while in strict violation of the prohibition by Jesus against marrying a divorced woman – a prohibition that, in the context of the divorce prohibition, echos the words of 18:20, *"Do not have carnal relations with your neighbor's wife and defile yourself with her."* But, no rational person would expect those who use the Bible to inflict harm to adhere to its rules.

It is a bit comical that we also have the Schumer Democrats approving of killing babies born after a failed abortion attempt – an act of infanticide equates to the sacrifice of a child or worship of Moloch, who is associated with child sacrifice. If people actually believed in the Bible, they would immediately recognize Schumer and Pence to be among those warned about at what Evangelicals refer to as "The End of Times" – which is actually simply a new age in humanity associated with the *"Age of Aquarius"* – the 2150 year progression of astrological age which moves the March, or vernal, equinox into a new constellation.

Assuming the star Regulus in the constellation Leo the Lion marked the ancient border between the constellations Leo and Cancer, the *"Age of Aquarius"* began in 2012, and coincided with the end of the Mayan Calendar.

Of course, those familiar with the Hippy Era Broadway hit, *HAIR*, will know the words: *"When the moon is in the Seventh House / And Jupiter aligns with Mars / Then peace will guide the planets / And love will steer the stars..."*

The Mayan saw it as a time when their culture would no

longer exist; the drafters of the *Book of Revelation* chose it as the final phase of mankind's evolution into a peaceful global culture that would understand and fully adopt Hebrew health and hygiene laws. We are seeing it as the last battle between those who oppose peace, health, and, of course, what the Bible defined *"spirit of God"*: *"Wisdom, Knowledge, and Understanding."*

One thing to understand is the universality of Nationalist sentiment which echoes that preceding every major war.

The other is the increased need for Universal Healthcare which we see openly opposed by the ultra-Right-wing with their "Most harm to the most people" agenda – an agenda Trump has disrupted, so, during the two week period defined by the end of his second 56 and 57-week periods, Trump came under fire from individuals, from both parties, who profit by harming others.

As Reagan put it, *"In this present crisis, government is not the solution to our problem, government IS the problem. It isn't so much that liberals are ignorant, it's just that they know so much that isn't so."*

One truth is that the incidence of colon cancer is on the rise among those under fifty-five. According to a 2017 study published in the Journal of the National Cancer Institute, those born after 1990 have four times the possibility of developing rectal cancer compared to someone born around 1950. This means that those who do not have Medicare are four times as likely to need care.

In order to inflict harm, the nation needs a President who is devoted to Right-wing theology. As such, elevating Mike Pence to the Oval defines their agenda and displaces any meaningful or real policy position proposals. If you say 'NO' without offering an alternative, your opponent is in the position of defending their position with nothing to attack or contrast with.

If Trump were a professional politician, this would pose a real problem. But, thanks to his ancestry, Trump is well trained and experienced PT Barnum – he's a showman who is well versed in distracting his target demographic while dropping the type of *'Easter Egg'* comment which will allow him to easily *'turn the stampeding herd.'*

With healthcare, it was when he said to Australian Prime Minister Malcolm Turnbull: *"I shouldn't say this to ... my friend from Australia, because you have better healthcare than we do."*

It was the perfect "no-lose" position. Trump is on record praising Universal Health and giving a boost to its Democratic proponent, Bernie Sanders – a man who is not a POTUS Cousin and, in an environment of growing global antisemitism, cannot win a Presidential Election. Even if antisemitism were set aside, he would turn 80-years-old during his first year in office, and that means voters must look at his potential successor as closely as they would him, and vote based on a Vice Presidential nominee.

Economically, by implementing the Australian system, the roughly 18% of GDP spent on U.S. Healthcare would be cut in half. Since more of that money is being shifted onto Medicare, there would be a clear gain in terms of the deficit. Actually, since the projected federal deficit for FY 2019 is 4.7% of GDP, the Budget would go into a surplus in excess of 3% of GDP.

Imagine the boasting Trump would do if he had a Budget surplus in excess of $580 Billion, the lowest unemployment rate in the nation's history, and retained the 71% economic approval rating, plus improved the Balance of Trade or the finalizing of an official end to the Korean War.

Whatever they might otherwise seek to accomplish, those who are attacking Trump must stop him from achieving anything that he could honestly own as his Official Presidential Legacy. In effect, Trump's opponents are no different than suicide bombers – they must destroy themselves, and the nation, before they can assert victory. Of course, the comedy comes from the fact they will be destroyed and not know if victory was achieved.

Just after the second 56-week period ended, Elizabeth Warren came out against the Electoral College – a Constitutional device designed to ensures the whole nation can exercise a voice in the selection of its President.

In the world of the Founding Fathers, nations were ruled by families who, for generations, emerged from single districts, shires or counties. The *"Electoral College"* ensured that all the voters, in every state – not just the most populous ones – had a voice in who would be the Chief Executive and Commander in Chief of the Military. Article Two of the Constitution defines the role of the electors in conjunction with the term of the President and their Vice President:

> *"Each State shall appoint, in such Manner as the Legislature thereof may direct, a Number of Electors, equal to the whole Number of Senators and Representatives to which the State may be entitled in the Congress: but no Senator or Representative, or Person holding an Office of Trust or Profit under the United States, shall be appointed an Elector."*

As the exclusionary phrases show, the Found Fathers sought to exclude the possibility of financial influence. However, we need to look to the Twelfth Amendment to see the clarification of the role of the Electoral College as ratified 15 June 1804, but one thing was certain: *"a majority of all the states shall be necessary to a choice."* ALL the states must decide, as opposed to what is, after Trump's defeat of Clinton, now argue that a few high population states should determine who occupies the Oval Office.

In an era when people are ranting about "elites" and how money is influencing politics, it is comical to observe the populist movement promoting the granting of control of the White House to those states which are the most wealthy and most influenced by the wealth of the *"One-Percent."*

In 2016, thirteen of the states Hillary Clinton won, had GDP in excess of a Billion dollars: California, $2,797; New York, $1,607; Illinois, $820; New Jersey, $592; Massachusetts, $528; Washington, $524; Virginia, $509; Minnesota, $351; Colorado, $343; Connecticut, $261; Oregon, $236; Nevada $156 and finally Maryland, $131. Of the remaining five states, whose combined population is less than the New York City metropolitan area, had GDPs less than a Billion dollars – New Mexico, $0.97; Hawaii, $0.88; New Hampshire, $0.81; Maine, $0.61; Vermont, $0.32.

For perspective, the first thirteen states have a combined GDP of $8,855 Billion, with the remaining states adding another $3.59 Billion for a total of $8,858.59 – against the United States 2016 GDP of $19.39 trillion, means they account for about 46% of the nation's Gross Domestic Product, while being on 36% of the nation. Therefore, Ending the Electoral College roughly equates to disenfranchising people in 64% of the States.

The founding fathers established the Electoral College in as a logical compromise between election of the President by a vote in Congress – what we might term a Parliamentary system – and election of the President by a popular vote of qualified citizens. As we now see, there is a vocal minority screaming for a move toward giving a handful of states control of the government.

Interestingly, because we are in the era of global Populism, we ignore history and the fact Trump is the fifth president elected contrary to the popular vote. The first was in 1824, when the son of President John Adams, John Quincy Adams, became the sixth person to hold the office. Then, in 1876, Rutherford B. Hayes was elected the 19th president; in 1888, Benjamin Harrison, grandson of the ninth president, William Henry Harrison, became the 23rd to hold the office.

Of course, the adults now ranting about Trump should be aware that, in 2000, George Walker Bush and those infamous *"hanging chads"* gave us the son of President George H. W. Bush, who destroyed the economy and began an undeclared that, as of this writing, is in its eighteenth year of Middle Eastern carnage. Bush-43 is also credited with signing the Patriot Act, which is the basis for the legal authorizing indefinite detentions of immigrants, and numerous things that effectively undermined human and Constitutional rights. Yet, he appears in the media and is treated with respect by those he sought to harm.

It is rather funny that the same media that denounces the Electoral College can also be seen attacking Andrew Jackson and wondering why Trump seems drawn to Tiffany's cousin. They fail to realize that, when running against Adams, Jackson won the popular vote by five times the percentage points of Hillary against Donald – meaning Jackson was extremely popular with voters.

Jackson offers the rational voter a meaningful lesson. He may have lost in 1824, but in 1828 he came back to win and held the office for two terms. Neither Clinton nor Sanders is about to win an election in 2020 – Hillary because she wouldn't risk it, and Sanders is just too old.

As was established early in the Mueller Investigation, the target demographic for Russian hackers was in the states Hillary won – the state with the broadest connectivity and social media access. This means, changing or circumventing the Constitution to weigh the outcome of the Presidential Election to those states is the same as empowering foreign propagandists in their effort to influence the election. This infers that Russia or some other "bad actor" is behind the drive to eliminate the Electoral College.

As history will doubtless prove true, as the nation moves closer to March 2020 nomination period, the idea that we should abandon the Electoral College, and deprive citizens of their voice, will prove detrimental to all who attempt to gain support from those voting in State Primaries whose rights will be lost in favor to the New York and California monied elites.

While that reality sinks in, voters will also be dealing with the idea of a "Constitutional coup" intended to install Mike Pence in the Oval. It has been heard before: After the assassination of JFK, it was deemed necessary to modify a portion of Article II, Section 1 to allow for a functionally incapacitated President. As Ratified on 10 February 1967, the 25th Amendment and included the provision:

> *"Whenever the Vice President and a majority of either the principal officers of the executive departments or of such other body as Congress may by law provide, transmit to the President pro tempore of the Senate and the Speaker of the House of Representatives their written declaration that the President is unable to discharge the powers and duties of his office, the Vice President shall immediately assume the powers and duties of the office as Acting President."*

If invoked, the President immediately lose their authority but retains the title. It's a lot cleaner than impeachment and sets the stage for a legal coup based on subjective opinion, as shown in the words of the husband of Counselor to the President Kellyanne Conway.

On Monday, 18 March 2019, George Conway, who is also an attorney, echoed the suggestion that Vice President Pence and the Cabinet should consider invoking the 25th Amendment and thereby remove President Trump based upon an alleged "mental condition" as evidenced by his PT Barnum style of controlling his target demographic.

Contrary to much of what has been proved accurate in this book series, Conway asserted, *"Don't assume that the things he says and does are part of a rational plan or strategy, because they seldom are. Consider them as a product of his pathologies, and they make perfect sense."*

There is always a time when the perfect storm of social and political emotion strikes. We have seen it in history, though we prefer to ignore it. Nationalism, popularism, antisemitism, mixed with religious fervor or antagonism in an environment marked by bigotry and stupidity in many forms – including an increase in drug usage. These are the making of the perfect storm.

But, there is also the underlying self-destructive behavior element. It has a perverted logic which those like Conway would never attack – they are too busy practicing it. The logic goes like this:

"If I can destroy what I have, I deny it to my successor and am no worse off than if I had never had it – with the benefit of having had it. If by nature or upbringing, I am passive aggressive I do this naturally and can adopt an air of honesty as I enter the state of denial about that which underlies my actions and serves as my motivation for those actions toward myself and others. Hurting us all equally."

As the Baby-boomers age, part of them harkens back to the days of Woodstock and smoking joints; another part has become the Conservatives they opposed in their youth. They come to learn why their elders reminisced about a horrible past as if it was an ideal time – because we can selectively remember the good times and the moments of happiness we shared with those who are no longer with us, they see the past being better than the present, and the mistakes that were made are easier to deal with or dismiss.

Curiously, they finally understand the words of the Beatles song, *"YESTERDAY"*

"Yesterday / All my troubles seemed so far away / Now it looks as though they're here to stay / Oh, I believe in yesterday / Suddenly / I'm not half the [person] I used to be / There's a shadow hanging over me / Oh, yesterday came suddenly..."

MAGA – "Make America Great Again" – the young look to history and ask *"When was it Great? When were things better than they are today?"* – the older generation looks back and says or thinks back to the days when they weren't worried about their health or the health of the spouse when their dreams were of the future and not their past. They are hearing from their children what Neil Young sang about in *"OLD MAN"*:

"Old man, look at my life / I'm a lot like you were / Old man, look at my life / I'm a lot like you were / Old man, look at my life / Twenty-four and there's so much more / Live alone in a paradise / That makes me think of two..."

Then there are the words of the late Harry Chapin, who was two years ahead of me and in my cousin's grade at Brooklyn Tech – *"Cat's in the Cradle."* It deals with the lost experiences of a father and his son, who, *"as he grew / He'd say 'I'm gonna be like you, dad' / 'You know I'm gonna be like you' ..."*

Dad's too busy to experience the joys of having his son and just can't seem to find the time. The boy grows, goes to college, gets married, has children of his own, and when dad, now retired, wants to spend the time, his son replies hasn't the time. *"And as I hung up the phone, it occurred to me / He'd grown up just like me / My boy was just like me..."*

In many ways, a part of our loss and self-destructiveness. It is what we want back, when we experience that wistful affection for days gone by and exhibit that sentimental fantasy for a period and people who instilled in use feeling of happiness – that is the "Great America" resonating in the souls of Trump's followers, just as, a generation ago, it did with Reaganites.

Politicians of Trump's generation and many of those who oppose him from the subsequent generations are really angry at what they've come to realize missed. Especially when we see the pictures of Trump with his grown children surrounding him.

Look at the media, where are the children of the politicians who are denouncing Trump? Do they work with their parents? Are they there, when there is no staged photo-op? The *"Cat's in the Cradle,"* but not among the Trumps, and that makes many of the professional Washington Swamp Denizens angry – especially since his kids all still have their *"silver spoon."*

Of course, the focus of attacks on the children is on Ivanka and her husband Jared Kushner – the only two who are Orthodox Jews. But it is consistent with emerging antisemitism and anti-Israel feelings among Democratic leaders.

CHAPTER SIX – Technique

"To sit home, read one's favorite paper, and scoff at the misdeeds of the men who do things is easy, but it is markedly ineffective. It is what evil men count upon the good men's doing"
~ Teddy Roosevelt, 21 December 1895

One need only look at the speculative attacks on Trump, to realize Teddy Roosevelt knew exactly what he was talking about. Mark Twain took a different and more personal perspective on the route to success, when, in 1887, he wrote: *"All you need in this life is ignorance and confidence, and then success is sure."*

Both men were actually saying the same thing. Roosevelt saw evil rely upon and benefit from the ignorance of the average person – something that manifests in their finding reasons to fail or finding fault with and attacking the alleged errors of those who achieve at a level that results in media finding it profitable to report every minor misstep. These are reported because they are blood substitutes – errors to be reported in accordance with the journalistic tabloid doctrine, "If it bleeds it leads." If there is no real blood, the Tabloid or "FakeNews" media will invent it.

Readers love injuries, they love to see others hurt, they gain great pleasure in attacking and bringing down the successful and those who actually take the risks that bring success as often as they fail. But only the failure is deemed newsworthy. So, if there is none, predict or speculate on it.

When Twain referenced ignorance, he was speaking of the same tendency taking hold inside of the head of an individual and is focused inward. Self-doubt, indecision, or negative attitudes, are the things which undermine our efforts.

Think how often have you said or felt you did not deserve something, that you weren't good enough, or maybe you could not approach another person because they were "out of your league"?

Deemed a leading expert in fitness and transformation, mindfulness, self-love, author Lori Hard expressed the idea that you should *"Except and expect positive things, and that is what you will receive."* And if we look at what Donald Trump is often attacked for, it is because he does exactly that. His detractors see evil to be kept as an enemy – Trump is negotiating improvements, thus he refers to them as friends or decent people. He always sees a deal or situation as good, except when he wants to ensure a response that distracts or spreads blood upon the waters to so the sharks will circle it – all the easier to eliminate them.

In some cases, like Climate Change, it pays to side with, to avoid, insulting your target demographic. This was shown by Hillary Clinton's "Basket of deplorables" characterization at her 9 September 2016 fundraiser – she later claimed was targeted at only half of Trump's base – insulting the opposition only rallies them and undercuts support critical to your primary objective. Hillary insulted those whose votes she needed.

Hillary based her entire campaign, her primary sales pitch, on being derogatory and dismissive of both Trump and his core Demographic. While Trump's approach, the hallmark of attacks, is a focus on specific individuals but not their supporters.

When dealing with Climate Change, Trump has said many things, some obviously sarcastic, others strategic. Consider when, on 29 Jan 2014, he tweeted. *"Give me clean, beautiful and healthy air - not the same old climate change (global warming) bullshit! I am tired of hearing this nonsense."*

Thirteen months earlier, on 6 Nov 2012, Trump blamed the Chinese, asserting, *"The concept of global warming was created by and for the Chinese in order to make U.S. manufacturing non-competitive."*

Naturally, when he is criticized for the obvious fallacy, his long history of negotiating with the Chinese and placing their mercantile heritage into perspective is ignored. People look at paper money and fail to realize it exists because the Chinese forced those seeking to do business with them to exchange their gold and silver for Chinese paper money.

The introduction of paper money or monetary certificates dates to the Spice and Silk Road trading era of the Tang dynasty, in the period when the Prophet Muhammad was alive, therefore it is as old as Islam. Bronzed shells or bronze coins have been dated to 1500BCE – Moses and the Exodus were 100-years later, in 1307BCE. With that historical context, Trump has long been critical of Chinese motives and methods and has been involved in a campaign criticizing Chinese trade practices – which dates back prior to a 21 September tweet in which he said, *"China is neither an ally or a friend – they want to beat us and own our country."*

The statement about Global Warming being a hoax can be seen as China making the Western nations debate something they were already addressing. Chinese laws require that all cars sold after 2025 be electric; they are reducing their reliance on coal and, at the same time, building ties with Middle Eastern oil producers. China leads the world in renewable energy sources; Western Nations waste time debating the degree to which humans have caused the changes seen over the past century – Bloody Stupid!

The *"concept,"* rather than the *"reality,"* is the hoax. What we can call observable reality is the melting of Arctic glaciers and the rise of sea levels driven by warming of the oceans. Trump can be sarcastic, as he was on 7 Nov 2012, when he tweeted, *"It's freezing and snowing in New York – we need global warming!"* And then repeated again on 25 May 2013, *"It's freezing outside, where the hell is 'global warming'??"* Which, on 14 Dec 2013, was followed with *"Wow, it's snowing in Israel and on the pyramids in Egypt. Are we still wasting billions on the global warming con? MAKE U.S. COMPETITIVE!"*

Has Trump attacked Tesla? Has he denounced California for experimenting with piezoelectric roadways, or the spread of wind farms? Of course not. He has even, rightly, suggested that the Border Wall would be ideal to combine with solar generating, *"There is a chance that we can do a solar wall. We have major companies looking at that. Look, there's no better place for solar than the Mexico border – the southern border. And there is a very good chance we can do a solar wall, which would actually look good."*

Those who allegedly want to address the causes of Climate Change immediately changed the subject to the cost of the Wall itself, and the current wholesale cost of electric. They actually argued, without specifically saying it, that we should continue to burn fossil fuels – because they are the source of the cited energy prices. The price analysis showed, *"with standard utility-scale solar installation costs as low as $1 per watt, the nearly 3 million panels would cost at least $1 billion. Even with the generous* *revenue estimate, it would take four years just to recuperate the installation costs of the panels."*

Nowhere was it mentioned, those same solar panels will still be installed at commercial production sites along the border. Nor do they mention the problems of finding appropriate sites and then financing those installations. But those sites aren't as good as the border location; in addition, it amounts to unnecessary duplication of work – there is the preparatory groundwork, the mounting for the collectors, access roads, and other unnecessary cost factors.

Trump's proposal would also expedite vital work to address Climate Change. In earlier books in this series, we addressed Trump's mention of his support for the coal industry, and "Clean Coal," even though coal use was decreasing. As mentioned, this was intended to tell existing miners their jobs were secure. On 25 March, it was reported that *"Coal is on the way out': study finds fossil fuel now pricier than solar or wind."* But, except for the new affirmation of the cost inversion which has made 75% of coal production more expensive, this was also previously mentioned. Now we know, by 2025, renewables should replace coal as a source of electricity.

Naturally, Trump's Border Solar Wall proposal would be dismissed – because Trump proposed it. Trump seems to have a grasp of the reality underlying his proposal. If we go with the estimate that, *"An area of solar panels 228 sq miles in a sunny part of the world could harness our entire global energy supply."* Then allow that half of that is access area or spaces between rows of collector panel, only 114 square miles is required – a distance of 114 miles one mile deep. The US-Mexican border extends about 1954 miles, which reduces that one mile depth to 388 feet; if we assumed the United States consumed a fifth of global energy, the distance is reduced to only 78 feet, or the equivalent of the fence placement relative to the actual border plus the access road, and the result is a fence that pays for itself to the same extent any other Solar Power Project does – with the auxiliary benefit of also controlling migration as intended in the 2006 Secure Fence Act.

One of Trump's typical techniques is to throw out ideas that others are promoting and see who is intelligent enough to grab hold and achieve their goal. Those who were upset by the exit from the Paris Accord, or who believe in renewable energy and reduction of the carbon footprint should, if their asserted beliefs are honestly held, have latched onto Trump's suggestion as the means to achieve their Green Energy goal.

But, since Trump proposed it, it must be rejected, then it is to be attacked and ridiculed. The only exception is when ignoring it will allow people to be harmed because hurting people canbe easily influenced by those promising to relieve their pain.

Those who do not understand might consider the attacks on the Affordable Care Act (ACA or Obamacare) which actually dates back to Teddy Roosevelt's failed 1912 presidential campaign.

As Trump indicated when praised the Australian system, Obamacare could be improved and governmental medical care services, such as those for Veterans, could be merged into it. On 26 March, the Justice Department agreed with the Federal Court ruling declaring Obamacare unconstitutional; this had the effect of reversing the administration's previous legal position as to the ability to separate unconstitutional segments and allow the law to stand.

Were Congress doing its job, the underlying issues would have been correct as soon as the possibility of voiding the law emerged. The record shows, as long ago as 26 March 2012, Trump had tweeted: "*ObamaCare is clearly unconstitutional. Hopefully the USC rules correctly but in the end repealing ObamaCare requires a political solution.*"

Trump correctly declared what the Federal Court has now affirmed, so on 14 December 1918, Trump was able to tweet: "*As I predicted all along, Obamacare has been struck down as an UNCONSTITUTIONAL disaster! Now Congress must pass a STRONG law that provides GREAT healthcare and protects pre-existing conditions. Mitch and Nancy, get it done!*"

Note that, unlike the Right-wing who would see America without healthcare, Trump has consistently called for providing better coverage – if only the congress who adopt an economically sound and rational approach, rather than continuing opposition that has defined the issue for well over a century. Trump's tactic is to take a long-term economic view, while also stirring the pot in a way that addresses the bias of his target demographic.

What we are really seeing with Trump's alleged *"Climate Change Denial"* is an example of his *"Turn the stampeding herd"* technique. To understand this, look at Pew Research findings on the matter: Consider, 70 percent of the sample group believe that Climate Change is real – which means a third of the population is in denial. By contrast, Pew Research published in 2018 found 67 percent of Americans believe a higher power (or God) that has personally rewarded them, and 25 percent say they talk to God and God talks back.

Add the 70 to 67 and you have a minimum overlap of 37 percent of the survey sample believing in both an interventionist deity and Climate Change. This then infers Climate Change is an *"Act of God"* and, as we see reports of species becoming extinct and look forward to the death of the Baby-Boom generation within a reproductive era of Negative Population growth, we can identify these beliefs with the Revelation predication that a third of life will die in this century. The dating of which can be found in the 2014 book, "*Biblical Prophecy: Are we in the Revelation Era.*"

We need to keep in mind that, the stampeding herd which Trump is attempting to turn are, to a significant extent, comprised of Republican Evangelicals and other devoutly religious people. In that context, if your religious belief system is predicated on an interventionist deity, and Climate Change is something that deity has determined would be allowed or made to happen, any direct action to stop it is tantamount to opposing the will of God – if you want these people on your side, you do not challenge their belief, rather you offer alternatives which will achieve your goals without directly confronting that belief.

If Climate Change is a Chinese mercantile hoax, it doesn't involve a deity; if the Wall can provide a renewable energy source that is desired and will otherwise be built, why not build it and thus achieve two goals for the price of one, simply by citing the desired one in a location where it will also serve dual purpose?

Of course, we see in those who take a NIMBY approach to renewable energy, while also opposing the Border Fence/Wall and wanting open borders, take actions to ridicule and attack both Trump and those who believe in interventionist deities. The effect is to create a divisive backlash which has all things secular being opposed and manifests in things like the anti-vaxxer movement.

While there are reasons to avoid some medications, the idea of avoiding vaccines and allowing diseases to spread, because of social media propaganda that has no scientific basis, is much the same as the motivation for Witch Trials in the late 1500s.

It is a harsh reality that humanity simply changes the focal point excuse, rather than the related action. Trump is saying this when you hear him yell about *"Witch Hunts."*

A *"Witch Hunt"* is a manifestation of basic mob psychology reactions to irrational or undocumented assertions intended to motivate attacks on a class of people. It can be the stereotype we associate with other races or a social class. It is routinely used when the modern media speaks of *"Elites"* and *"Oligarchs."*

The goal is to create either a class or individual who can be hated with some degree of impunity – because, as much as those doing it will deny it, humans need to *"hate."* Hatred and exclusion are a way to ensure the evolution process works – a mutation occurs and becomes the basis for the segregation of those with and without it.

In both cases, reproduction continues with the mutation confined to one group – if it is a beneficial mutation, that group prospers and the basis for the "hate" grows to the detriment of those not carrying the beneficial mutation. Some mutations are visible, others internal, and still others seem to carry subliminal triggers that we instinctively respond to. Trump, like every other president over the past 230-years, seems to carry the latter.

We all are aware of the *epicanthic fold* which defines the Asian eyes, a subtle variation of which has been identified among the Irish. We know that a pigment called *melanin* causes tanning and distinguishes Caucasian from Negroid based on the intensity of the sun in their native ancestral environments. What an anti-vaxxer doesn't seem to be aware of – when they blame vaccines for *autism* – is that many people with autism do not produce enough melatonin, which also regulates sleep (our circadian rhythm also called our biological clock).

Challenging the anti-vaxxer propaganda, we know Autism Spectrum Disorder (ADS) affects 1 in 59 children in the U.S. and is 4-times as prevalent in males; it is also associated with reduced IQ among about a third of those having it – from 1980 to 2000,

ADS has declined by roughly fifty-percent, with the rates varying between states and therefore between genetic pools within the population. This is confirmed by family and twin studies which show some people have a genetic predisposition to autism – if one is affected, between 36 to 95 percent of the time also be affected the other one.

The anti-vaxxer premise of vaccines being a cause ignores evidence of parental or genetic family characteristics presenting as mild impairments in social communication skills and/or abnormal repetitive behaviors. Emotional disorders – bipolar disorder or schizophrenia – are more common in those families and reflects upon the rational abilities of anti-vaxxers.

These three examples are visible elements of evolutionary separation, and how ignorance can then cause harm to the society in the same way superstitions and *"Witch Hunts"* can. They also present characteristics of target demographic populations which can be manipulated for political gain. Those opposing Trump seek to capitalize on segregation mentality – the hatred for "the other" which is critical to the evolution of the species.

Then there is the *"subliminal"* element which, in terms of American presidential politics, underlies the genealogical aspects of the 2017 book *Jonathon's POTUS Cousins*, which are linked to a pattern called *"Assortative mating."*

For some *"subliminal"* or other undefinable reason, every American Presidents has been a descendant of at least one of the five daughters of the 6th Earl of Chester, who was a descendant of William 'The Conqueror' King of England & Duke of Normandy.

It is a weird coincidence and one that carries the pattern of economic strength or weakness based on whether or not the real leadership conforms and complies with that lineage – the stronger the connection, the stronger the economy and government.

In that context, of the potential Democratic nominees for President in 2020, we have a 38-year-old Army Major, who served in Iraq, Congresswoman Tulsi Gabbard, who enjoys twice Donald Trump's connectivity.

We also have former Vice President Joe Biden and Senator Elizabeth Warren, whose ancestry duplicates Trump's. Since they meet the subliminal historic criteria, their successful candidacy would revolve around their campaign positions. On 12 March, Joe Biden indicated he intended to run, but was still structuring his campaign strategy and as the period covered in this cycle came to an end, Biden was a front-runner who had yet to formally declare he was in the race. Meanwhile, Elizabeth Warren was already on the campaign trail – possibly putting both feet in her mouth.

In this cycle, we can dismiss most of the potential nominees as non-POTUS Cousins and therefore losers who, if nominated would lose and if elected, would reveal if the break from history is relevant to the survival of the nation. We can make an exception for John W Hickenloope, who has 50 percent more connectivity, and William F "Bill" Weld, who also has twice the connectivity and therefore is as strong as the female candidates.

Trump's media control technique requires him to attack the individual who is the least threatening but attracts the greatest media attention. For that reason, attacked Warren – thus raising her profile at the cost to media presence of candidates who could prove a serious competitive threat.

Bernie Sanders is not a threat and enjoys the benefit of a false post-election claim that he could have won where Hillary Lost. Like Bernie, Hillary Clinton is not a POTUS cousin within the context of the common ancestry, but she is within the context of *Jonathon's POTUS Cousins*. That distinction explains Hillary being among the five who won the popular vote and yet lost the Electoral College and therefore the Presidency. That said, the loss by those five was not a conscious decision to exclude non-family. But the Electoral College was designed to filter candidates so as to ensure strength of leadership is the highest possible between the choices – that means the popular vote within each of the States must accept the leadership of the one occupying the Oval Office.

As mentioned, part of Trump's technique is to attack those who are relatively meaningless but will generate media coverage.

Concurrent with the filing of Mueller's Report, Trump was again badmouthing the late Republican Senator John McCain. As a deceased Republican, McCain offers no political blowback, but is the perfect vehicle to get the media ignoring events so they can devote time to praising McCain and denouncing Trump for his *"cruelty"* and *"aching need for attention and the pathetic pose of toughness.*"

But the fact is, all history will recall is the wealth of praise for McCain. It will become part of any future biographies, and the statements by Trump will be ignored. We know the game, it was alluded to on 23 January 2016, when Trump stated, "*I could stand in the middle of 5th Avenue and shoot somebody and I wouldn't lose voters.*" Figuratively, he is shooting McCain – but not the way George W. Bush did during the 2000 primary when McCain was very much alive.

Bush-43 had no problem spreading rumors that McCain had fathered the Bangladeshi child he and his wife, Cindy, later adopted. Bush also claimed, when McCain was a prisoner of war, was a traitor, or some form of *Manchurian Candidate* Benedict Arnold, whose wife was also a drug addict.

Where Bush defamed McCain and apparently lied about Cindy, Trump has said, "*He's not a war hero. He's a war hero because he was captured. I like people that weren't captured.*"

On 9 February 2017, Trump Tweeted, "*Sen. McCain should not be talking about the success or failure of a mission to the media. Only emboldens the enemy! He's been losing so...*"

As we know from the second Korean Summit, the ongoing derogatory talk directed at Trump by media based Comedians and Congress didn't "*embolden*" Korea so much as it made it difficult to deal with key issues. Effectively the process was undermined by the mindless speculation surrounding discussions of Mueller's Russia investigation.

With the release of Mueller's report, we saw the psychology of *The Emperor's New Clothes*, where the mob rejects the facts and continues to insist it sees what it was told it should see. This mentality was reflected in the words of Democrat Chris Anderson, who, on 24 March and prior to the release of Attorney General William Barr's summary of the Mueller findings, said, "*Barring a bombshell revelation, voters are likely to view the report through the prism of their partisan identities.*"

As was revealed, almost immediately upon the news that Barr's reading of the key points in the Mueller report, taken in the context of there being no basis for indictments, was that Trump had been exonerated from any participation in historic pattern of

Russian activities prior books in the series showed CIA memos affirmed dated back to the Kennedy era.

Though there are now far more important issues to deal with, the Swap Denizens in the Democratic Party are continuing their impeachment or criminal indictment tactics to undermine the government. It would be comical if, thirty or fifty years from now, historians discovered an element of those Denizens were in the pay of Russia or some other nation actively seeking the fall of America. One issue to be dealt with is BREXIT.

The clock on the cycle for this book is ticking into Brexit and the range of problems the European Union must deal with – without the benefits of Britain. While America's leaders focus on inventing reasons to impeach Trump, Theresa May is at the center of the wave of frustration which is about to overwhelm leaders of the 27 European Union countries.

That frustration reflects the lack of true economic growth over the past 25-years. The Eurozone has the same Baby-Boom and NPG problem facing both Japan and America, except that the world-class companies which define the EU economy are every bit as old as its Boomers. Volkswagen, the recovery vehicle of the Third Reich, and then consume automotive leader, has newer facilities in American than in Germany.

We are now entering the fourth Industrial Revolution – a revolution build upon emerging technologies defined by artificial intelligence and robotic, which Trump has said he wants America to promote, and which are already advanced in China and Korea. But the EU has none of it. There is no European Amazon, like New York City, Europe seems to have no interest in the economic engine it represents. There no Google or Facebook. There is no equivalent of either Skype or the Chinese WeChat.

China is an innovative growth market which America needs to position against, Europe has fallen behind and its economy actually depends on an influx of American money that is America's NATO contribution. When we hear about the Balance of Trade and American Trade Deficit, Americans fail to grasp the realities that are consuming the eurozone, where Germany depends on its export-dominated economy that is a victim to the global economy.

The recession everyone was saying would impact America

at the end of 2018 or beginning of 2019, almost hit Germany, but it did bring growth to a near halt with eurozone growth holding around 0.2% – about a tenth of the growth rate "experts" said would befall America. But, the "experts" were wrong and figures show the second quarter of 2018 had real GDP growth of 4.2%, followed by a third-quarter growth of 3.5%, while real disposable personal income increased 2.5%.

If we look to Italy we see a nation that has been hit hard by the usual cyclical recessions, complicated by the compounding problem of illegal immigration. The same problem Trump seeks to prevent via the Wall, but Pelosi and Schumer are attempting to exacerbate to the point where it will both negatively impact the Trump Legacy and the American economy.

Due to the lackluster ability of the eurozone to adjust to economic variables, Italy has become one of the first EU nations to align with China's Belt and Road initiative and reflects the type of act of economic desperation that China seeks to capitalize on. Again, Trump's trade war with China takes on importance as the difference between becoming a minion to China or equal partner in an economic system defining the 21st-century – a century in which the old colonial nations are marginalized.

Here's where the problems with Elizabeth Warren arise.

As our cycles created their activity period, Warren declared, if elected president, her administration would treat the American giants of the global tech industry – Amazon, Facebook, Google – as if they were simple domestic monopolies and break them up.

The matter progressed into 2007, when Economist Milton Friedman posited the very thing Warren has asserted she would seek – increased government regulation of an industry relatively free of government intrusion, with the result that technological progress would be impeded.

By doing so, Warren would undermine what is effectively American dominance and allow China to become a global high-tech monopoly with the resources to dictate internet usage and control. Warren's declaration alluded to the Sherman Antitrust Act and various lawsuits against Microsoft which first manifested in a Federal Trade Commission 1992 complaint about an alleged monopoly on the PC operating system market. You should note that this attack on Microsoft was concurrent with China's leader, Deng Xiaoping, announcing his intention to initiate economic reforms which culminated in *The New Silk Road* and the *Socialist Market Economy* which is better described as Biblical Capitalism of the Old Testament variety.

Prior to the 19th-century British disruption of the Chinese economy, China had held its position as one of the world's largest and most advanced economies for two thousand years. With the Deng Xiaoping policy change, it only too a decade for the private sector to provide half of the nation's GDP and continue growth at a solid rate toward world dominance – until Trump confronted them and halted their "*real annual gross domestic product (GDP) growth averaging 9.5% through 2017.*"

In the 1990s, when China had yet to adopt the return to its Biblical Zebulon-Issachar socialist-capitalist government model, Warren's attitude might have some minor merit. But American high-tech firms are now competing against Chinese IT developers who were trained at the best universities in America. Therefore, China enters the competition on an equal intellectual footing with their American counterparts. The main difference is that they are adherents of the Zebulon-Issachar model – a Capitalist Merchant class provides support needs of the academic scholarly class, and the combined effect is national prosperity.

In the American context of the derogatory "Socialist" label bandied about by closet anti-Semites, is the false identification of the dictatorship style called which called itself Communism with the Biblical idea that Intellectualism and Scholarship should be fully supported both socially and economically. Were there people in America who actually understood the Bible, they would be known through their promotion of free education combined with financial support for scholars and their families funded by some percentage of international trade revenue.

Warren's position is diametrically opposed to the nature of the Chinese system which sees a monopolistic integration of high-tech elements to the point where, rather than using plastic credit cards, Chinese consumers pay via their smartphone, which, of course, has all the digitally integrated functions associated with 4G and computer connectivity. Plus, China is already on the road to the next level or generation of communication technology. That is, the level Trump detractors said was fantasy when, on 21 February 2019, Trump Tweeted, *"I want 5G, and even 6G, technology in the United States as soon as possible. It is far more powerful, faster, and smarter than the current standard. American companies must step up their efforts, or get left behind. There is no reason that we should be lagging behind on........."*

As was pointed out at the time, Sprint and T-Mobile were in the process of getting authority to complete their $26-billion merger; their justification is that they need to partner in order to deploy 5G nationwide. Until that deployment is completed, and its operational characteristics can be observed, 6G remains only a theoretical next generation grandchild.

With the merger completed, in January 2019, the New T-Mobile announced the 5G rollout would result in 7,500 more customer care professionals being employed by 2024 than would have existed under the stand-alone companies – 5,600 of those jobs would be in place by 2021, and these are in addition to the 12,000 new jobs New T-Mobile expected would be created to serve small towns and rural communities, and all are a direct result of the merger.

The integrated functions are exactly what Warren wants to break-off into lesser and independent corporate entities. If she were successful, the ability to uniformly upgrade products would disappear. America would not be able to produce the broad-based platform offered by the Chinese conglomerate *Tencent* – creator of *WeChat*. Every software update or improvement would take months or even years to become uniformly integrated into various "independent" software applications, and, by the time they are, they would still be rendered outdated by every subsequent update to security and other functions in the master operating system or hardware.

As part of its *New Silk Road*, there are high levels of tech investment being made India and Africa, where mobile payment systems have growing importance. Effectively Warren wants to cripple American competitiveness and hobble the ability of High-Tech American competition at a time when Trump is attempting to establish a level of competitive equality.

Warren's approach would have prevented the creation of

the T-Mobile jobs, weaken American communication growth, is why she is an easy target for Trump and explains why he wants her to receive media attention through his attacks on her.

Domestically, monopolies can eliminate competitors and harm can the economy. They can also develop a new market to the point where it is profitable and thereby stimulate competition from those who are unwilling to risk their resources on unproven markets. In the Global arena, National monopolies are exactly what a nation wants – as early as Roman times, China had it with Silk and Spices; the British Empire can be attributed to the State approved monopoly known as The British East India Company.

Anti-Trust actions are predicated on the idea of stimulating competition, by creating multiple companies within an otherwise monopolistic market. Of course, the competitive idea and goal is to "win" – or control a market, to have a defacto monopoly. When a firm is broken up, it simply sheds the least profitable segments and declares them "competition." This was seen and experienced when the breakup of the Bell System was mandated on January 8, 1982, which was then followed by an evolutionary pattern which involved liquidation of debt-liabilities as the newly created firms "reorganized" under various bankruptcy procedures, effectively gaining tax benefits.

Trump's technique is predicated on using the law, rather than breaking it. Those seeking his impeachment, like those who sought to impeach Bill Clinton and George W Bush, requires the invention of improper behavior.

This is true even when, as with Bush, there might have been solid reasons to impeach. The underlying problem of an honest impeachment process or investigation is that it exposes all those engaged in criminal or improper behavior. We saw this with the Russian Interference Investigation – numerous indictments and convictions of fringe members of prior administrations.

Now, Trump gets to weaponize the report and galvanize his base, and allow the "Collusion Truthers" to self-destruct.

CHAPTER SEVEN – Ramifications

"Anyone who has never made a mistake has never tried anything new."

~ Albert Einstein

Ramifications, the rule of unintended consequences, they can get interesting and we see why Trump fights back when he is attacked. Case in point, Stormy Daniels, attorney, who used the fining of a lawsuit as a means of circumventing a non-disclosure agreement. When Michael Avenatti did that, he made it a point to garner all the publicity possible, and by so doing made that NDA moot.

Having gained national attention, he decided to capitalize on it by announcing as a presidential, possibly getting campaign donations, and seeing where it would go. But, when you receive national publicity, it draws attention to everything else you do. So it was that on Monday 25 March 2019, Avenatti was arrested on charges of fraud and attempted extortion relative to Nike Shoes – with other charges involving embezzled a client's money to pay off personal debts, and a bit of bank fraud involving phony tax returns.

As we know, his little case against Trump resulted in his client having to pay about a quarter of a million dollars to cover Trump's legal fees when they lost their case. Those who sue Trump, and see him fight back, tend to forget he grew-up in a home that produced a respected Federal Judge, and had become a millionaire at the age of three because his father knew how to read and use the law. Trump has, for decades, profited by having people underestimate his intelligence.

Then there is the ramifications for Avenatti's target, Nike. With his arrest Avenatti began a multi-day twitter storm repeating the same promise or threat: *"I will fully cooperate with the NCAA to my maximum ability. Names, dates, amounts, texts, emails, bogus invoices, bank records, wire payments, cash payments, etc. - ALL OF IT. Let's talk about the truth and facts of what really happened and let the chips fall where they may."*

The basis of Avenatti threat was a breaking news revelation

about wealthy individuals bribing individuals to obtain admission to elite colleges for their children. The dominoes are falling. And when someone has little to lose but everything to gain, they can make a real mess.

There are ramifications to those who have opposed Trump and called for his impeachment even before the Inauguration.

Since Pelosi knows these ramifications transcend simple politics, she has, on a pragmatic basis, effectively admitted her choice would be to deprive the nation of security and crash the economy, rather than allow Trump to receive credit for the next critical phase in the Secure Fence Act – which, based on the statistics Trump presented in the Oval Office meeting, was a great 'Democratic' success. A success that both she and Schumer seemed to toss away out of spite.

Pelosi even went so far as to mention the enormous cost of Ted Cruz forcing a 17-day shutdown over ACA. She, therefore, made it perfectly clear that she understood the enormous cost of not giving Trump the border security Democrats once fought for.

At 11:49 AM - 13 Dec 2018, Pelosi foolishly played into Trump's hand when she Tweeted: *"At a time when there is so much uncertainty about the economic security of working families, it is deeply disturbing that @realDonaldTrump is threatening a #TrumpShutdown. This is far from the treatment American families deserve during the holiday season."*

To say, *"I will take the mantle"* is to say you will wear the clothing, it is not taking credit for being the tailor or designer. If credit is given where credit due, voters will recognize that Pelosi and Schumer decided to harm them, rather than grant Trump a wall easily be funded by following the Bernie Sanders suggestion to double income subject to Social Security contributions – which would flood the Treasury coffers without impacting the economy.

A few days after the Oval Office meeting, author Charlie Kirk posted a video on Twitter which presented certain "facts" of relevance to the Border Wall discussion – if they prove true: *"The annual cost of illegal immigrants is over 115 BILLION in benefits; 10,000 kids are trafficked across the border annually 98% of all heroin comes across the border."*

Based on those numbers, by denying Trump $5 Billion for

the Democratic Fence he calls a Wall, Pelosi, and Schumer decided it was better for the nation to spend twenty-three times as much for a stopgap prior to the inevitable flood of immigrants who will be driven north as Climate Change affects equatorial regions.

We also have the local hypocrisy of a government seeking open borders and an influx of undocumented workers – people who will wait years for the hearings where they might be declared legal. In December 2018, New Jersey began looking at the Trump Golf Course and workers employed using forged Social Security numbers and other phony documents – a universal practice which must increase as Reagan Democrats eliminate border controls.

To achieve there goal, they passed a Continuing Resolution which held spending at existing levels and politically passed the problem off to the newly elected Congress, where the House would be controlled by the Reagan Democrats like Beto O'Rourke, whose first announced legislative objective was to end Federal Eminent Domain for the purpose of immigration control or border security.

At 10:28 AM on 20 Dec 2018, Trump inferred that there would be no shutdown. He claimed to have signed the Continuing Resolution, tweeting: *"When I begrudgingly signed the Omnibus Bill, I was promised the Wall and Border Security by leadership. Would be done by end of year (NOW). It didn't happen! We foolishly fight for Border Security for other countries - but not for our beloved U.S.A. Not good!"*

Twelve hours later, at 10:20 PM, Trump Tweeted: *"Soon to be Speaker Nancy Pelosi said, last week live from the Oval Office, that the Republicans didn't have the votes for Border Security. Today the House Republicans voted and won, 217-185. Nancy does not have to apologize. All I want is GREAT BORDER SECURITY!"*

The change came with the introduction of an amendment by Rep. Paul Ryan authorizing $5.7 Billion for Secure Fence Wall, and, despite Pelosi saying such a bill would never pass the House, as Trump noted, it easily passed with a 217-185 vote.

The Reagan Democrats decided they would invalidate the 2006 Secure Fence Act and advocate the open borders proclaimed by Ronald Reagan in his 1980 campaign.

Trump had Tweeted an indication the matter was settled,

then there was a meeting with the outgoing House Speaker, Paul Ryan, who then returned to Congress, rewrote the legislation to include $5.7 billion for the wall and the threatened Shutdown was back in play.

At 11:39 – 21 December, a White House tweet stated:

"The Senate has a choice to make: Keep America's borders open to those with no regard for our laws, or secure our border and keep the Government open and working for the American people.

It's straightforward, it's common sense, and it's urgent."

Democrats had an opportunity to improve Social Security, secure the border against the Climate Change migration which should be seen over the coming decades, and possibly even raise the Minimum Wage to above poverty. But that opportunity was not one the wished to avail themselves of. In the Senate, Schumer would choose to oppose his own documented positions on illegal immigration and close the government. A fact he declared on the Senate floor when he effectively declared war on both Trump and his own historic position on illegal immigration, by saying:

"In a short time, the Senate will take part in a pointless exercise to demonstrate to our House colleagues and the president what everyone here already knows. There are not the votes for an expensive, taxpayer-funded border wall. So, President Trump, you will not get your wall. Abandon your shutdown strategy. You're not getting your wall today, next week, or on January 3 when Democrats take control of the House."

This the same Chuck Schumer who supported $25Billion for "Border Security," but has made it clear he was really a Reagan Democrat who opposed his own 2006 legislative success – and prefers Reagan's open border policy over rational asylum seeker crowd control. To underscore his Right-wing Reagan allegiance, we look back to an interview two months prior to the shutdown, when Schumer refused to endorse a single-payer medical system known as Universal Medicare. He hedged his political bets by saying:

"Look, Democrats are for universal access to healthcare, from one end of the party to the other. We want more people

covered, everyone covered; we want better healthcare at a lower cost. People have different views as to how to get there. Many are for Medicare for All, some are for Medicare buy-in, some are Medicare over 55, some are Medicaid buy-in, some are public option. I'm going to support a plan that can pass, and that can provide the best, cheapest healthcare for all Americans."

But, as Schumer established with the Government Shutdown, it only takes ten members of the Senate to prevent anything – even funding for legislation their leadership had promoted a dozen years earlier when it was politically beneficial for all to make-believe they were interested in secure borders.

As Trump Tweeted at 12:10 PM – 24 Dec 2018, *"The Wall is different than the 25 Billion Dollars in Border Security. The complete Wall will be built with the Shutdown money plus funds already in hand. The reporting has been inaccurate on the point. The problem is, without the Wall, much of the rest of Dollars are wasted!"*

Schumer boldly laid claim to the Reaganite mantel of fiscal irresponsibility which had been the exclusive property of the ultra-Right-wing recession creators. Accordingly, the closing Bell for Xmas Eve welcomed a DJIA Dow Jones Industrial Average which, at 21,792.20 – down 653.17 points (2.9%) – was on the cusp of being a Bear Market, before rebounding to close the week 2,500 points higher.

In the background, there was the questionable ruling that zeroing the mandate had rendered Obamacare unconstitutional, and "Wall Street Democrats" already fighting the Republican war against the possibility of Bernie Sanders running in 2020. In a campaign donation email, Sanders pointed out "They not only want to discourage or defeat a Sanders candidacy, they want to make sure that the progressive agenda is not advanced by anyone." The "They" in question being both Chuck Schumer and the "Wall Street Democrats" – both of whom seem happy to have adopted the Reagan agenda.

Apart from supporting a Democratic border barrier that we know was opposed by Ronald Reagan, Trump had been calling for National Healthcare superior to that of Australia – which would be Bernie Sanders' Universal Medicare... going into 2019, the issue was the Democrat leadership's willingness to turn Reagan Republican rather than allow Trump to win on traditional issues and goals of the Democratic Party.

The Trump technique involves allowing the other guy to blame you for their screw-ups, and then relying upon objective observers to place the blame where it rightfully belongs. History will record that Trump destroyed the Right-wing by holding them close, and Democrats by encouraging them to evidence the same irrationality Republicans demonstrated with their Birther claims.

At 8:02 – 17 Dec 2018, Trump tweeted, *"The DEDUCTIBLE which comes with ObamaCare is so high that it is practically not even useable! Hurts families badly. We have a chance, working with the Democrats, to deliver great HealthCare! A confirming Supreme Court Decision will lead to GREAT HealthCare results for Americans!"*

Six minutes later, at 8:08 AM, Trump Tweeted, *"Anytime you hear a Democrat saying that you can have good Border Security without a Wall, write them off as just another politician following the party line. Time for us to save billions of dollars a year and have, at the same time, far greater safety and control!"*

The billions saved are the support costs that are now falling on Tijuana and are already a reality with regard to illegals already in the States. If Trump is wrong, then the 2006 Secure Fence Act was wrong and should be repealed; if he is correct, the act is on the books and should be properly funded, even if Trump insists upon calling it a 'Wall" rather than a "Fence."

Then, twenty minutes later, at 8:28, Trump posted, *"It is incredible that with a very strong dollar and virtually no inflation, the outside world blowing up around us, Paris is burning and China way down, the Fed is even considering yet another interest rate hike. Take the Victory!"* A possible change of subject, but a point that needed to be raised – even though he refrained from including BREXIT (a possible character restriction determined omission).

On 4 January, day-one of the new Democratic House, they voted 239-192 for a short term bill to end the shutdown. There was no chance the Senate would support it, and no possibility of it escaping a veto. Speaking on Fox News, vice-president Pence declared, *"The president has made it very clear: No wall, no deal! We're here to make a deal, but it's a deal that's going to result in achieving real gains on border security, and you have no border security without a wall. We will have no deal without a wall."*

As members of the media pointed out, what was evolving into the longest government shutdown in history, was a dispute over $5 billion in a $4.4 trillion budget.

More importantly, this dispute involved the Democratic leadership stubbornly refusing to fund improvements to their own 2006 Secure Fence Act. And, as the news reported, the dispute was for an amount which was 40% below Apple's misestimate of projected Chinese earnings from sales of its new $1000 iPhone. Basically, Schumer and Pelosi were demonstrating they were petty self-hating politicians devoid of any rational sense of proportion. It was evidence of gross incompetence which threatened to define their legislative agenda and, ultimately, threaten the nation.

As the Democrats once knew, without barriers, the border is open for any who wish to enter the nation. This raises questions about who gains from borders which vehicles can easily cross and thus carry into the country any contraband they wish. Who gains and who is in collusion with them – is Schumer conspiring with someone to smuggle items across the Southern border?

It certainly might seem that way, why else would he refuse funding his own 2006 and 2013 legislative agenda?

And, possibly more important is the fact that the Schumer shutdown in opposition to funding his own legislative program is over an amount roughly the equivalent to the monthly cost of SNAP (Food Stamps) – which, due to combined failure to produce an annual budget and joint failure to even submit a Continuing Resolution for the funding of a program which annually feeds 42 million Americans, has resulted in a loss of funding which would take effect in February 2019.

Schumer's attack on his own Bush-era legislative agenda was apparently worth threatening starvation to the 68% of SNAP recipients that are families with children. To spite Trump, and attack his own legislation, Schumer proudly threatened children with malnourishment. And, of course, if his effort to stop the

Wall/Fence improvements were to succeed, tens of thousands would cross the border and need to be supported by SNAP – or some related program – until such time as they could legally work. Thus, Schumer was fighting to increase the annual SNAP budget by an amount approaching the cost of the 'Wall/Fence' he fought to have in 2006.

The economics of the shutdown resulting from Schumer's obstruction of his own legislation clearly establishes how Reagan Democrats have adopted the destructiveness of Reaganomics to fit the gullibility of their demographic base. A simple increase in the Minimum Wage to 150% of poverty would eliminate enough people from public assistance to cover monthly funding of the 'Wall' or any infrastructure program in a similar cost bracket.

In a Tweet on Saturday, 5 January, we saw Trump make a veiled reference to the Secure Fence Act: *"V.P. Mike Pence and team just left the White House. Briefed me on their meeting with the Schumer/Pelosi representatives. Not much headway made today. Second meeting set for tomorrow. After so many decades, must finally and permanently fix the problems on the Southern Border!"*

The reference *"After so many decades"* refers back to 1980, when Ronald Reagan was opposing border security and promoting open borders providing unrestricted travel to any who enter via Mexico, regardless of nation of origin or reason for migrating. Under Reagan's plan, smugglers would no longer need to smuggle they could just bring the contraband in. Inherent in the reference is a reaction to Reagan policy objectives – laws which kept the borders secure and sought to make them more secure, laws that included those Fence, Wall, and Barrier Laws of 1996 and 2006.

In the world of leadership, you do NOT back down, you do not reverse yourself ... unless you gain more by that reversal than you could possibly gain by stubbornly going forward. Trump can gain by backing down; Pelosi can only lose and loses even more when she refuses to back down.

In that context, we also need to ponder what does Senator Schumer gain when he is attacking the Border Wall/Fence he and his fellow Democrats worked over three decades to pass into law? This was the same Fence that Obama had declared completed, when, factually, only a third of the structure had been built, but his reference was to the initially funded segment – so, if the era of Trump "Lie" criteria is applied, Obama blatantly lied, but if reality is applied to both, we have both men asserting contextual truth.

In the televised portion of a private White House meeting between President Trump and Vice President Pence, Schumer, and Nancy Pelosi, the nation had witnessed Trump smile and say: *"And then we have the easy one, the wall. That will be the easiest of all, what do you think Chuck?"* Only to have Schumer justify denying funding for his own legislation with a sternly delivered: *"It's called funding the government."*

Granted, the funding they were discussing includes about $1.3 billion for fencing and other security measures at the border as part of The homeland Bill. But it is clearly insufficient in terms of stopping illegal entry of Caravan migrants. In addition, funding lacked the multi-billions needed if the "open border" faction were to win the debate and achieve what Ronald Reagan had argued for in 1980, and Schumer now appeared to be arguing for in 2018.

Only days before the White House meeting, Conservative Judge Jay Bybee wrote a 65-page decision in which he effectively asserted the Reagan position by ruling Trump lacked a legal basis to issue a proclamation that would deny illegals the right to claim asylum and send them back across the border.

Ten days after Trump's Proclamation – On 19 November, an Obama appointee, U.S. District Judge Jon S. Tigar, halted implementation of the Trump order.

With both judges declining to secure *"the integrity of our borders,"* the nation watched as the Caravan migrants lifted their children over or through the border fence. It was clear that the Federal Court had decided border integrity was not a Presidential concern and the Caravan migrants had a choice between entering illegally or awaiting processing in Tijuana.

With the matter one of Reagan-Democrat verses everyone else, the world witnessed a 35-day partial shutdown of American government services – labeled the longest in the nation's history. It only ended when Trump seemed to "blink" – an action which prevented the collapse of the Food Stamp Program and security dangers serious enough to force closure of various key airports.

Factors which neither Pelosi nor Schumer even noted or cared about.

At that point, the Political types entered into negotiations to formally settle matters before a critical budget crisis do to occur at midnight on 15 February. On 12 February, the Associated Press reported a settlement and *"that the accord would provide $1.375 billion to build 55 miles of new border barriers."*

Of course, that still required a formal written draft and the President's signature, but it would fund the government until the September end of the Fiscal Year and would allow Trump time to make the Wall a 2020 Campaign issue.

Concurrent with the accord being reached, Trump held a rally in the border town of El Paso, Texas, where he stood below a banner declaring *"Walls save lives."* Only hours before, Trump had released a campaign video, called "El Paso Residents: Finish the Wall, It Kept Us Safe," which contained repeated testimony and references to verifiable facts in support of the fact that crimes had dropped significantly since completion of the Obama Wall. It was now an issue of "Finish the wall" – finish the wall which had been authorized by the 2006 Secure Fence Act that Schumer had supported and Pelosi opposed.

At exactly the same time, Beto O'Rourke was holding a rally where he was proclaiming *"Walls end lives"* – but his claim was a philosophical one, where Trump's claims that they save lives could be supported by the dead bodies of those left to die in the desert by human trafficking *"coyotes"* whose living was derived from the on smuggling people across unsecured border regions.

O'Rourke was clearly concerned with voters and had no concern for women and children who died of thirst or exposure in the deserts. For Trump, while the accord only provided funding for about a quarter of the 215-mile addition to existing structures, it was a victory – it fully funded what could be built and made operational before the 30 September end of the 2019 fiscal year.

If we harken back to a c-span video of Schumer speaking on the Senate Floor, where he is welcoming $6Billion for the Border Security he was opposing in 2018, and doing so with words from June 2013:

"Fewer illegal immigrants, higher GDP, more jobs, reduced

*deficits. Who could oppose that? I don't know of anybody …
if they care about America."*

Of course, at a time before there were caravans of migrants
seeking both legal and illegal entry, Schumer also asserted, *"We let
people cross the borders, millions, who take jobs away from
workers."* But, in 2019, Schumer and Pelosi were fighting to allow
them to cross.

Schumer once held, as stated on the Senate Floor in 2013:
*"We are committed to ending the waves of illegal immigration
that we've seen in the last 30 years…Crossing the border without
permission from the government is a crime."*

Those were in conjunction with a 68 to 32 vote in the U.S.
Senate marking passage of what was termed to be a landmark
overhaul of immigration laws and top item on Obama's agenda.

Senator Marco Rubio said, *"This proposal mandates the
most border and interior security measures in our nation's
history. For example, it requires and funds the completion of
700 miles [1,126 kilometers] of real border fence. It adds 20,000
new border agents. It details a specific technology plan for
[monitoring] each sector of the border."*

Consider these facts: In 2006, Congress authorized and
partially funded construction of 700 miles (1,125 km) of physical
fence/barriers along the Mexican border. Then, in 2013, Senators
passed S.744 the *Border Security, Economic Opportunity, and
Immigration Modernization Act*, and the House killed it; for two
years, it was blocked by Republican House Speaker John Boehner.

Based on Congressional Budget Office data, the Center for
American Progress calculated the cost to the nation would average
$37 million/day or $26.8 billion over those two years when the
Republicans obstructed the 113th Congress legislation Chuck
Schumer had sponsored. But then things changed, Trump was
elected and supported the goal of Schumer's legislation, and he
brought the Republicans into line behind it – Schumer switched
sides and, in 2018, began to vehemently oppose what had been his
own long-standing legislative objectives.

We now have the fun of wondering just how expensive the
Schumer-Pelosi obstructionism will prove to be. And, obviously,
they decided to run a tab that includes the Mueller investigation

– per an @GOP Tweet on 24 March 2019, *"The total reported cost of the Special Counsel's investigation through September 2018 was $25,215,853.00."* On 25 March, Rudy Giuliani updated the estimate, saying it "*cost actually about $40 million.*" But, as of April 2019, the costs were still being booked and represent a significant cost to state what had been known for decades – Russia messes with American elections and has kept pace with changing technologies. But we can cover those ramifications in the Mueller chapter, where we find reason to think the Russians really wanted Hillary to win, but, since they couldn't manipulate the Electoral College, their goal was thwarted.

As the administration approaches the end of its second 57-week period, we need to ask and honestly address the real issue of, What has President Trump done that has hurt the country?

The honest answer would be NOTHING!

And that's what's being used to attack him – the fact that he is a proven successful salesman. He's so successful that, as a Republican, he utilized a decades-old Democratic platform, then proved, if presented in terms they understood, it could rally the Republican demographic base.

Where the Right-wing wanted to dump Obamacare, Trump repeatedly asked that it be improved – and the Democrats ignored him, then, effectively, recommended the exact same thing – on 25 March, speaking at a CNN town hall event, Senator Kamala Harris stated the current system revolving around the private insurance industry was "*inhumane*" and should be eliminated, that "*we need to have Medicare for all.*"

Of course, Kamala Harris is one of the non-POTUS Cousins seeking the 2020 Democratic nomination. She is echoing Bernie Sanders position, and yet, with a Democratic-controlled House, cannot seem to the necessary leadership to have the House initiate its version of *"Medicare for all"* legislation. It's the same problem Senator Bernie Sanders has – Congressional members of their Party aren't paying attention to them, and everyone is ignoring the fact that Trump would likely back intelligent *"Medicare for all"* legislation. Any Democrat who could get a Republican President to back their legislative initiatives would win popular support.

However, as Harris promoted rational healthcare, Schumer

was giving the Republicans political gifts, by waging war against a member of his own Party, Representative Ilhan Omar, because Israel's Prime Minister, Benjamin Netanyahu had replied to one of her tweets with the line "From this Benjamin: It's not about the Benjamins!" – which was a play on the title of a Puff Daddy song, "*It's all about the Benjamins baby*" that Omar seems to have used to explain the reason underlying a few of Israel's objections to some Obama policies.

Of course, "Benjamins" is a reference to money, specifically $100 bills on which Benjamin Franklin is depicted. And in Puff Daddy's song, he effectively utilizes the classic stereotype, saying, "*You should do what we do, stack chips like Hebrews / Don't let the melody intrigue you, 'cause I leave you / I'm only here for that green paper with the eagle.*"

Comically, as a Jew from a family whose ancestor was the daughter of the famed 10th-century scholar called The Rashi – Rabbi Solomon ben Isaac (Shlomo Yitzhaki) – I would think there is some merit in saying money influences all decisions. And the use of Puffy Daddy saying "*I'm here for the money*" and emulating the Hebrews – as we know the Chinese have proven extremely successful by emulating the Hebrews and America would be wise to also emulate Issachar and Zebulon.

As for any anti-Semitism on the part of Ilhan Omar, at 2:22 PM on 26 March she tweeted, "*That is why two of my first acts as a Member of Congress were to co-sponsor a bill elevating the position of Special Envoy to combat anti-Semitism—and my first op-ed after my election was on the rise of hate crimes.*" It is interesting that while the Senate version, S.238 - Special Envoy to Monitor and Combat Anti-Semitism Act of 2019, was introduced by Republican Senator Rubio, Marco on 28 January 2010, Schumer's name is absent from the co-sponsors, which include Senator Warren and Senator Gillibrand.

It would appear Schumer has no interest in the purpose stated in Sec.3.a.3: appointing an envoy whose duties include "*combating anti-Semitism and anti-Semitic incitement that occur in foreign countries.*" Could the Republicans be correct when they asserted that there was an element within the Democratic Party that was anti-Israel? Is Schumer the pot calling the kettle black – is he the real anti-Semite of the group, and is his racist bigotry the reason he attacked Omar? Is that persistent and stupid looking smirk on his face caused by his belief that nobody has caught on to his true nature and motivation?

GOOGLE political lies and you get quotes like this, which might well describe Schumer: "*Are you a politician or does lying just run in your family?*" – Fannie Flagg, Fried Green Tomatoes at the Whistle Stop Café"

When it comes to detecting liars, one needs to look at what Trump opposes. He has attacked NAFTA and trade agreements which were initiated and negotiated under Reagan, then signed by Bill Clinton. He is, in fact, attacking Reaganomics.

Reagan advocated open borders and instituted amnesty, while also opposing the border Wall or Fence that the Democrats eventually enacted under Bush. But, when Trump accepted the Democrat's illegal immigration position, the Democrat leadership went whole-hog on both its Reagan-like support for amnesty and Reagan opposition to its own 2006 Secure Fence legislation being properly funded and effectively designed. They even appear to have adopted a Reaganomics approach to trade.

If you don't get it, Fannie Flagg was saying politicians lie, it is what they do for a living. Not being a professional politician, it is easy to chastise Trump for playing the politician and beating them at their own game. In reality, Trump is simply functioning as a salesman speaking to his target demographic. This involved adopting Reagan's #MAGA slogan and the Democrats fence/wall to create a broad base sales pitch.

Trump was castigated for saying he gets legal advice from watching TV and pointing out that, "*Michael Cohen plead guilty to two counts of campaign finance violations that are not a crime. President Obama had a big campaign finance violation and it was easily settled!*"

In a related quote, legal scholar Alan Dershowitz stated: "*I have been teaching and practicing criminal law for more than a half century, and yet, I have to acknowledge that I am having difficulty understanding the laws as they relate to the allegations made by Cohen against President Trump.*"

In a media interview on 26 August, California Democratic Congressman Eric Swalwell made it clear his party was unlikely to pursue any immediate impeachment related hearings. While he was clear in acknowledging there was insufficient factual data to justify impeachment, he didn't hesitate to attack the president by saying:

"We don't want to be as reckless with the facts as he is. I think having thorough investigations, putting forth an impenetrable case, doing it in a bipartisan way is the proper way to do this, but we're not there yet."

He did, however, tell ABCNews that his party *"promised the American people if we are given the majority,"* they would then conduct investigations the GOP was unwilling to conduct. Which was interesting, given the fact Robert Mueller was a Republican and all the convictions obtained up to that point were obtained through the efforts of the Republican Administration.

This could only mean that the attention would be turned from investigating over five decades of Russian interference in the American electoral system, and refocused on specifically attacking the President in the same way Richard Nixon was investigated – an investigation, accompanied by a 45% decline Stock values, but did not culminate in impeachment or prosecution.

Phrased in terms of 2018, this would mean undoing the Obama Recovery and resetting the markets to their 1999 levels. In effect, Swalwell's statement could be seen as promising to erase all the proceeds from Baby-Boomer retirement investments. This was something Trump would not respond to, because Swalwell was playing Trump's game.

However, he made a point of saying, *"Democrats should not lead with impeachment, George. I think we should lead with the core issues people care about, making sure that health care costs go down, that their paychecks go up, and that we scrub out corruption. But we shouldn't look the other way."*

Trump's technique includes a "Game Theory" strategy that is based on the Golden Rule, and known as "Tit for Tat." Often it is expressed in terms of "The Prisoner's Dilemma."

The Golden Rule, which is universal to all ancient cultures, tells us we should do to others as they do to us. The "Tit for Tat" strategy begins with the instruction that your first move is to be cooperative with your competition; from thereafter the strategy is to mimic your opponents' actions. This was clearly apparent in the dealings between Kim Jong-un and POTUS Trump, as readers know was described in the TRUMP CARD book series published between April and September 2017, and equated to a schoolyard pissing contest.

If your opponent cooperates, you cooperate, belligerency is answered in kind, and if they then cooperate, you exhibit the act of forgiveness and again cooperate. Aggression meets aggression, but with forgiveness always on the table. Trump is seen to attack someone and then say something nice about them. When he finds a positive, he is expressing or demonstrating "forgiveness" in the context of strong aggression being something he is comfortable with.

This drives the media pundits crazy. They cannot handle the type of behavioral gradients which are normal to negotiations in real-world, long-term, situations. Their whole economic model is built on asymmetrical information – knowing something that is important or audience grabbing that their competitor does not know. When we talk of transparency, we are really saying that all data must be available in a symmetrical manner – internet search engines are supposedly based on symmetrical algorithms which produce results in a "best fit" or most searched order, which then allows you to modify your query to tailor responses to your needs.

The media thinks in terms of news cycles, politicians think in election cycles. Trump was raised and trained to be a real estate businessman – one who invests for decades, not the hours, days, or weeks which comprise a news cycle. A politician comes into office with the realization that, unless he acts to create something the voters can see immediately, he will be removed in two, four or six years. The politician has no vested interest in the children and grandchildren of voters – unless those voters force them to care.

The job of the Tabloid media is to ensure the voters do not think about the future. The last thing a Tabloid wants is a reader who relates to a story on a practical level. That story must trigger an immediate emotional reaction or the media will avoid it. That makes the media the enemy of the people – an enemy which has a Constructional right to expose or conceal information in order to manipulate public opinion.

Trump appears to approach things in the way Muhammad Ali (Cassius Marcellus Clay Jr) described fights are won or lost: *"The fight is won or lost far away from witnesses behind the lines, in the gym, and out there on the road, long before I dance under those lights."*

When listening to Trump, think about the words of Helen Keller: *"Optimism is the faith that leads to achievement. Nothing can be done without hope and confidence."* Trump exudes the timelessness of the affirmative approach Keller was speaking of. We see this whenever Trump says something is "The Best" or "The Greatest", and is attacked by alleged "Fact Checkers" who would prefer to hear how bad things are or will be. Yet, the evidence in negotiations with North Korea would imply Trump's positive spin works.

On 23 January, in the midst of the Government Shutdown, the game Kim and Trump were playing took a turn, with Trump sending Kim a letter, and Kim publically responding his intention to trust President Trump's approach toward diplomacy going into a summit between the two planned for late February.

KCNA, the North Korean News Agency, reported: *"Kim Jong Un said that we will believe in President Trump's positive way of thinking, wait with patience and in good faith and, together with the U.S., advance step by step toward the goal to be reached by the two countries."*

On 9 February, as Trump prepared for the next phase of the Summit, Congressional negotiations broke down and it looked like the nation would, on 14 February, again face a partial shutdown. In a Fox News interview, acting White House chief of staff Mick Mulvaney phrased it very simply, *"The president is going to build the wall. That's our attitude at this point. We'll take as much money as you can give us, and we'll go find the money somewhere else, legally, and build that wall on the southern border, with or without Congress."*

In the meantime, Pelosi and Schumer were pushing the idea of decreasing the number of detention beds from 40,520 to 35,520 – replacing Federal beds with ankle bracelets and Federal support for the detainees with local community welfare programs, until such time as their cases can be heard. Decreasing the beds would certainly not decrease the numbers crossing the border illegally, and setting them free in communities could encourage them.

As President Trump phrased it, *"I don't think the Dems on the Border Committee are being allowed by their leaders to make a deal. They are offering very little money for the desperately needed Border Wall & now, out of the blue, want a cap on convicted violent felons to be held in detention!"*

As phrased by House Budget Committee Chairman John Yarmuth, *"I think the big problem here is this has become pretty much an ego negotiation. And this really isn't over substance."*

The problem being the irrational egotism was on the part of Pelosi and Schumer. And, as the childish ego-play continued, the Governor of California announced the withdrawal of National Guard troops from their positions along the California-Mexico border – an action which would invite additional illegal crossings.

As the next shutdown drew near, there were few willing to speculate or even consider how the childishness would reflect on Trump's second summit with North Korean leader Kim Jong-un in the Vietnamese capital Hanoi, on 27-28 February.

Clearly, it was important to evaluate Trump's handling of Congressional egotistical stupidity against the normal Trump Technique aimed at persuading North Korea to completely halt further development of nuclear weapons programs – programs of importance to the national ego to the people of North Korea.

It has been said, if you care what people think, they own you. In Asian culture, everything is about what people think; it's about *"Saving Face."*

For true peace, a real end to the Korean War, Trump must ensure the North Koreans *"Save Face."* That means they must be perceived as the dominant force, even while Trump is pulling the strings. There are multiple forces in America working overtime to embarrass the President and the Nation. The Ramifications of their success will, like the sins of the fathers, be felt unto the third or fourth generation.

A ramification tested in the 2020 Election? Will America, for the first time in its history, fail to elect a POTUS COUSIN?

CHAPTER EIGHT– POPULATION

"The leadership are fooling themselves. Overpopulation is a very serious problem, and over immigration is a big part of it. We must address both. We can't ignore either."

~ David Brower, Outside Magazine, July 1998

Both the national and global the populations have entered the post-Baby-Boom rebound cycle – the pendulum is swinging in the other direction – we need to realize and accept this. When we look at Trump's rejection of the Paris Climate Accord, we see that he has, either instinctively or intellectually realized the underlying reality that Global Warming aspect of Climate Change is directly correlated to population growth.

The correlation is derived from the average per capita use of fossil fuels as a "constant," meaning that, as the population grew, but continued to use antiquated heating in poorly insulated homes, the level of atmospheric gases generated grew.

Many individuals challenge the correlation between their numbers and Global Warming, generally because, as Millennials or younger Gen-X, they fail to consider how rapidly technologies have changed since the 1970s – when telephone service in rural areas of the nation still had "Party lines," homes were heated with wood or coal, and many people still depended on the Town Well for their drinking water. As for home computers, there was the Radio Shack TRS-80 Model I released in 1977 and the Model III released in 1980, with all of 64K of memory, at a starting price of $700 {$2,150 in 2019 dollars}.

In a Capitalist Free Market economy, both individuals and industry strive for the cheapest most efficient means of meeting their needs. With computers, memory, and applications, everyone reading this can attest to advances made since 1980 – at the dawn of the Reagan Era.

Capitalist Free Market activities have revised the electric car, which, in 1900, were 38% of the automobiles in use. Henry Ford and Thomas Edison were collaborating on an electric vehicle in 1914. Edison is reported asserting: "*I believe that ultimately the electric motor will be universally used for trucking in all large cities and that the electric automobile will be the family carriage of the future. All trucking must come to electricity. I am convinced that it will not be long before all the trucking in New York City will be electric."*

But the electric car could only travel 90-miles on a charge and electric transmission was still centralized around major cities – which meant the gasoline-powered version was more practical.

That Free Market practicality, combined with population growth which also started in earnest during that turn-of-the-century era, contributed to Climate Change.

With the availability of clean renewable generation in the form of inexpensive solar or wind power, electric cars have once again emerged as an economically practical and environmentally friendly alternative to gasoline-power. And what is not discussed in the media is the fact that petroleum reserves are depleting, and the reliance on fracking is evidence that oil-producing nations are scraping the bottom of their collective barrels.

The Saudis and other high reserve petroleum economies will soon be the only suppliers – recognized the long-term benefit to having an alternate and renewable energy resource to replace depleting oil reserves, they are protecting their reserves by moving to renewables. Of course, being desert nations, Middle Eastern oil-producing nations are ideally situated for solar. They also seek nuclear generation – so they can develop nuclear weapons under the protective cover of using nuclear to meet their electric needs.

Any nation which continues to rely on petroleum will, by 2030, become a slave to the Saudis, Iranians, and Russians. But, in terms of population and climate change, that does not matter.

In August 2001, in written and oral testimony to Congress, the Sierrans for U.S. Population Stabilization (SUSPS) detailed a population-immigration-environment connection. In that report, SUSPS stated: *"The United States, at a population of over 291 million, is the world's third most populous country, after China and India, and has the highest population growth rate of all industrialized countries."*

As the most industrialized of the three highest population nations, we can understand why the U.S. would also produce more atmospheric gases than either of the other two nations – we should also understand, given Chin's eye toward dominating this century, China is seeking to focus its development in a renewable energy context, and, within that context, has mandated all vehicles sold after 2025 must be electric powered, while concurrently ending its reliance on coal.

Those who consider long-term military vulnerability have, either instinctively or intellectually, realized decentralized energy supplies are more easily defended. While it might require the "defenders" to be disbursed – rather than tightly concentrated in a traditional Roman formation or concentrated in some form of fixed fortification configuration.

Dispersing domestic forces means an aggressor must also divide their invasion force; they must multiply supply lines and support services so as to wage attacks over a broader area. In the era of the missile and drone, it still forces multiple attacks before their activities begin to have any effect. When, on 13 April 2017, Trump ordered the use of a MOAB {Mother Of All Bombs} against an ISIS affiliate in Afghanistan's eastern Nangarhar Province, he demonstrated the inherent problem of the military training and base facility – he killed all the enemy soldiers without any civilian casualties.

While this idea is phrased in military terms, on a day-to-day peacetime basis, it means a storm or accident cannot disrupt the overall energy grid. As we know, Global Warming and Climate Change carry with it the reality of more intense tropical storms, and therefore the probability of situations like that experienced by Puerto Rico in 2017, which was still uncertified in 2018, with the after-effects still being felt in 2019 and possibly into 2020.

Climate Change is a direct result of environmental change caused by a combination of human activity and normal geological activity – such as the eruption of Hawaii's Kilauea volcano in May 2018. That eruption was part of an ongoing cycle which began on 3 January 1983.

The human activity component began in the late 1800s, as the industrial age really kicked in and new technologies like automobiles began to accelerate the use of combustible fuels, while people retained their old fossil fuel based energy activities.

As a result, climate warmth increased in direct proportion to the population growth. We've now hit the evolutionary point where the use of fossil fuels is, like a reliance on slaves was in the 1860s, economically counter-productive.

In terms of population growth, we have fertility or birth rates and immigration. In the oral portion of the SUSPS report to Congress, Sierra Club chairperson Bill Elder stated: *"For almost 200 years (1776 through 1965) immigration averaged about two million per decade."* He also informed them that, *"Our 1990's growth of 33 million exceeds that of any other census decade in our nation's history."*

During the final weeks of the period we are dealing with, President Trump declared the Border situation an "Emergency" justifying the construction of a wall to stop illegal immigration, the flood of illegal addictive drugs, and human trafficking. To place this in perspective, in both 2000 and 2005, apprehended illegals numbered over 1.5 million individuals – that is, in one year as many people were stopped and arrested at the border as had legally entered the country in each of the 19-decades from the birth of the nation to the year when the last of the Baby-boomers was born.

Elder went on to underscore the economic reality: *"Thirty three million is equivalent to adding a state the size of California - including all its houses, apartments, factories, office buildings, shopping centers, schools, streets, freeways and automobiles - its consumption of power, water, food and consumer goods -- and its entire waste stream of refuse, air and water pollution - to an already crowded and stressed U.S. environment."*

On 29 March, a representative of the Border Patrol and ICE told the reporter that monthly apprehensions had already reached 120,000 and the border detention and processing resources were already stretched beyond their design capacity. Annualizing the current trend meant we had returned to the 1.5 million mark twice achieved prior to passage of the 2006 Secure Fence Act.

Of course, given that in mid-October 2018, discussions and debates leading into the Midterm Election saw the inclusion of the immigrant caravan heading from Guatemala to the US-Mexican border. By Thanksgiving, an estimated 7,000 people – adults and children – had arrived in Tijuana where they could expect a six-month wait for an appoint to present their case for asylum. As they settled in, former First Lady Hillary Clinton was in Europe and was quoted saying that Europe is *"not going to be able to continue to provide refuge and support,... if we don't deal with the migration issue it will continue to roil the body politic."*

That use of "roil" – to make muddy – fits the situation for migrants to both Europe, yet we were lead to believe it did not describe the Mexican-American border problem which Elder had testified, during the period when Clinton and Obama were both Senators, was, in its immigration context, an environmental issue.

It is also worth noting that, at the time of Senator Barack Obama had said: *"We simply cannot allow people to pour into the U.S., undetected, undocumented, unchecked and circumventing the line of people who are waiting patiently, diligently, lawfully to become immigrants in this country."*

This, of course, sounds just like President Trump, who has been known to plagiarize ideas. And, of course, he gets attacked by those who accepted those same ideas from the original source, or, as in the case of Chuck Schumer, were the original source, and so, are effectively attacking themselves.

The crux of the matter is not about denouncing those who enter illegally from Latin America – fools quickly accept its about racism, when there is a reality they seek to avoid. Moreover, it can be called racism when Trump advocates border security, but not when Obama did it. It is, after all, about the race of the speaker.

But let us go back to the Clinton Administration and ideas now associated with Climate Change and the Green New Deal. In July 1998, the late David Brower – considered one of the most influential environmental leaders of the last century – was quoted, in *Outside* magazine, expressing the opinion: *"The leadership are fooling themselves. Overpopulation is a very serious problem, and over-immigration is a big part of it. We must address both. We can't ignore either."*

In May 2000, six months prior to his death at the age of 88, Brower told the San Francisco Chronicle: *"The world is burning and all I hear from them is the music of violins...Overpopulation is perhaps the biggest problem facing us and immigration is part of the problem. It has to be addressed."*

The population problem for the United States is different from that of the global population. However, for Republicans like Utah Senator Mike Lee, it's a joke, something to made fun of when attacking those who are concerned about Climate Change. In his attack on Congresswoman Ocasio-Cortez and the Green New Deal, on 26 March 2019, Lee tweeted, *"The solution to climate change is not this unserious resolution, but the serious business of human flourishing – the solution to so many of our problems, at all times and in all places: fall in love, get married and have some kids."*

As with those who oppose abortion, Lee seeks to make the effects of Climate Change worse for America. It's a variation on a *"Most Harm To The Most People"* agenda which underlays all far-Right-wing policies and defines the actions of those promoting the *Dump Trump* movement which seeks to replace Trump with the Theocratic Right-wing Mike Pence.

Before we explore the numbers that make population such a critical issue, let's cite some end of cycle warnings issued by Trump.

He has threatened to close the Mexican border to all traffic. If we think about this in terms of the Wall/Fence and its effect on illegal drugs, those opposing the Wall have been quick to point out that most of the drugs are smuggled through *Ports of Entry*. thus, if we are to stop the drugs, we must close those *Ports of Entry*.

The act of doing so will not only allow America to address the growing addiction problem but will create economic pressure on the Mexican government to address the real issue of migrants passing through its territory. It will also deprive the drug cartels of the money used to bribe Mexican officials – while saving many American lives which would be lost to addiction, but, without the access to drugs, will go into withdrawal and receive treatment.

Concurrent with the border closing threat, Commissioner Kevin McAleenan of the Customs Border Protection {CBP} service revealed the scale of apprehensions had reached a point where the agency was performing "direct release" of detained migrants – that means, Immigrations and Customs Enforcement officials no longer have the option of deciding whether an individual can be accepted into custody or needs to be released pending a court hearing, the release "will happen more expeditiously and directly," because it will be made by a CBP agent. In defense of the change, he said, *"That is not something we want to do. It is something we have to do given the overcrowding in our facilities."*

Congress has a choice, pay a few Billion dollars for a Fence or Wall, or authorize tens of Billions to increase migrant housing and process the millions of migrants who will be driven north by social collapse and Climate Change.

On 30 March, Obama's Department of Homeland Security Secretary Jeh Johnson stated that the large number Central and South American migrants apprehended had reached levels which might necessitate a repeat of the 2018 family separation crisis: *"We might be at the doorstep of another separating families type of crisis. The idea of sending a 7-year-old back to Central America without due process is something that most Americans should have serious objections to. There are other ways to deal with this situation right now."*

Under Obama, where there was ongoing construction of the border fence and verbal warnings regarding the consequences of illegal entry, the highest monthly apprehension rate had been the 65,000 people detained in May 2014. But, referencing the March figures, Johnson stated, *"We're on pace, this month, for 100,000 apprehensions. So this is a crisis. It's very definitely a crisis."*

Of course, Trump had previously stated it was a crisis and, over Congressional objection, issued an Emergency Declaration to address it.

Repeating his reference to unaccompanied children, which Obama had stated, without any outcry, would be sent back across the border, Johnson emphasized, *"There are ways to deal with this, there are answers — there are no easy answers — the one thing that we should not do, as Americans, is send a 7-year-old, an 8-year-old, an unaccompanied child back to Central America without due process."*

As to the causality, he went on to say, *"What is driving this and how do you address it? Very clearly, what is driving it now are the continued underlying conditions in Central America, the poverty and the violence there. That is always an overwhelming factor in illegal migration, and there's no level of border security that you can throw at that problem to act as a complete deterrent, as long as the underlying conditions exist."*

Naturally, such comments are to be ignored, because they are reflected in Trumps 4:36 PM, 30 March 2019, comment on his Twitter account: *"Mexico must use its very strong immigration laws to stop the many thousands of people trying to get into the USA. Our detention areas are maxed out & we will take no more illegals. Next step is to close the Border! This will also help us with stopping the Drug flow from Mexico!"*

The Cardinal Rule for the start of the 2020 election cycle is and shall remain: *If Trump says it, argue it is a lie and argue that the opposite must be done, even if he is expressing goals that are in full agreement with your previous positions and the prior administration.*

Democratic House leader Nancy Pelosi, the touchstone for pro-Republican campaign commercials, was clearly credited with adopting the Cardinal Rule, when, in March 2018, Gridiron Club Dinner cast members parodied her with a variation of a song from the 1933 Marx Brothers film "Duck Soup": *"I don't know what Trump has to say / "It makes no difference anyway / "Whatever it is, we're against it / "Even if our own side once professed it "We're against it."*

We know Obama's comments were little different from those of New York's Senator Chuck Schumer. With the coming of Trump, the positions shifted and those on the Left are echoing the 1980 campaign positions put forward by Ronald Reagan – these were decidedly anti-fence, pro-amnesty, and, in terms of workers, open border.

On 9 November, a San Francisco federal court judge even went so far as to deny that the president has *"broad discretion to suspend the entry of aliens into the United States,"* and seemed to rule those willfully or flagrantly violating American border law were still free to claim asylum because this was implied by the Immigration and Nationality Act, or INA, which maintains that if a person — even if they've crossed the border illegally — is, upon setting foot on U.S. soil, eligible to apply for asylum.

In his ruling, U.S. District Judge Jon S. Tigar even said:

"There is no justifiable reason to flatly deny people the right to apply for asylum, and we cannot send them back to danger based on the manner of their entry. Congress has been clear on this point for decades."

So it would seem that claiming asylum is a defense against a willful violation of American law which does not oppose asylum seekers entry via a lawful port of entry. Moreover, it secures the rights of such a claim to any who crash through border security.

Just after Thanksgiving, Mexico's new president, Andrés Manuel López Obrador, who built his entire political career on defending the poor was confronted by the reality of the Caravan migrants waiting in Tijuana for appointments to request asylum in the United States – they cost Tijuana over $26,000/day in food and minimal basic necessities.

President Trump decided to test how firmly Obrador was devoted to his political rhetoric of helping the poor and his fellow Mexicans. Since this was only a tentative first wave or prelude to the coming Climate Change migration, would Obrador seize the opportunity to create an infrastructure that can handle them, or would he fold and expose himself as a low-grade politician and not worthy to be a 21st-century leader?

Trump clearly stated, *"Here's the bottom line: Nobody is coming into our country unless they come in legally."*

Utilizing Twitter, he made it clear it was Mexico's problem to handle as they would, and the one thing that was certain was, *"...they are NOT coming into the U.S.A. We will close the Border permanently if need be. Congress, fund the WALL!"*

In 1993 Senator Harry Reid and complained that, *"In 1986, we granted amnesty—and I voted against that provision in law—we granted amnesty to 3.2 million illegal immigrants. After being in this country for 10 years, the average amnesty recipient had a sixth-grade education, earned less than $6 an hour, and presently qualifies for the earned-income tax credit."*

In 2017, there were 542,000 workers earning the federal minimum wage of $7.25 per hour; in 1993, the decade year Reid referred to, the minimum wage was $4.25, which means that $6 equates to $10.25 in 2018. Which means he denigrated everyone who doesn't live in Massachusetts, Washington, or New York City.

Reid then framed his attack on Birthright Citizenship: "*In 1993, in Los Angeles County, at Los Angeles County Hospital, one of the largest hospitals in the country, 67 percent of the births were to illegal alien mothers. The State of California needs to build a school a day to keep up with the incoming immigrant children–a school a day.*"

Of course, on 1 November, an Ivanka Trump Tweet pointed out that, "*For the first time in history, we have more vacant jobs than we have unemployed workers to fill them.*" And if we think back to Reid's Senate Floor comment, those babies would be 25-years-old and the educated American workers needed to fill those vacant positions.

So, what was Democrat Harry Reid was saying, when he set the rhetorical agenda for the Trump era Republicans? What was he thinking when he said:

"If making it easy to be an illegal alien isn't enough, how about offering a reward for being an illegal immigrant? No sane country would do that, right?

"Guess again. If you break our laws by entering this country without permission and give birth to a child, we reward that child with U.S. citizenship and guarantee a full access to all public and social services this society provides. And that's a lot of services."

"Is it any wonder that two-thirds of the babies born at taxpayer expense at county-run hospitals in Los Angeles are born to illegal alien mothers?"

"No sane country would do that, right?"

Was the Nevada Senator actually arguing to create a worker shortage, when, 22-years later, the first Baby-boomers turned 70?

At a time when 1 in 13 births are to illegal immigrants, it is an inescapable reality that excluding them only worsens the real long-term effects of NPG. As our schools empty out, instead of building *"a school a day to keep up with the incoming immigrant children"*, communities are closing schools and consolidating their school districts.

When Donald Trump echoes Reid, what is really happening is that he is pointing out the harmful policy Reid had promoted with S.1351, *"Immigration Stabilization Act of 1993"* – defined as

"A Bill To curb criminal activity by aliens, to defend against acts of international terrorism, to protect American workers from unfair labor competition, and to relieve pressure on public services by strengthening border security and stabilizing immigration into the United States."

When denouncing the criminal element mixed in with the illegals, Trump is simply restating Reid's August 1993 comment: *"Even worse, Americans have seen heinous crimes committed by individuals who are here illegally."* But, those now attacking the Democratic position espoused by Reid, now espoused by Trump, seem to be denying that those smuggling drugs are criminals.

Twenty-five years later, the far-Left Democrats denounced Trump for espousing Reid's legislative goals, while simultaneous repeating those advocated by Ronald Reagan in 1980. There is no center in politics, there is only a pair of opposing pendulums that happen to pass each other at varying points deemed to be common ground, centrist, or bipartisan.

But, partisan politics dominates the issue of population and climate change. It is an area where being partisan is also being a Denizen of the most disease-infested political Swamp. Worse, the bigoted and narrow Cold War mindset of the last century shaped a political establishment which works hard to ignore demographic and technological realities which are defining the 21st-century.

The demographics are based on population and citizenship – the very things which justify the need for a census. A reading of Article 1, Section 2 shows it specifies enumeration of "Persons" via a decennial census and provides for the flexibility of additional information by stating it shall be conducted *"in such Manner as they shall by Law direct."*

The first census, in 1790, simply listed the name of the head of each household, the number of free white males under the age of 16 and the number older than 16, number of free white women, other free persons, and slaves – all basic demographic data. In the next census, and thereafter, they started to breakdown the groups into age-ranges and then, each person was identified by age.

The first census of real value to genealogists was in 1850, and included details of the individuals which included their name, age, place or country of birth, occupation, education, health, and race – White, Black, or Mulatto; slaves were listed by owner, with no individual name identification. Was the person literate, what was their occupation or trade, did they own property, and what was the value of their personal estate?

After the Civil War, in 1870, there are questions about both citizenship and right to vote. A decade later, the questions were expanded to include the birthplace of parents and marital status. From there on out, a citizenship question was implicit or explicit – was the person "naturalized," an "alien," year of immigration?

In 2010, questionnaires used between 1940 and 2000 were replaced by a single form having 10 questions, including one that asked if the person was of *"Hispanic, Latino, or Spanish origin."* In addition, there was an American Community Survey (ACS) that included the traditional questions, asked on an annual basis, with no household receiving the survey more than once in a five year period.

It's May 2006 *Design and Methodology* Technical Paper 67 states: *"Like the decennial census, the ACS interviews the resident population without regard to the person's legal status or citizenship."* However, this does not mean citizenship status is excluded. Some questions are *"used to determine the U.S. citizen and non-U.S. citizen populations and to determine the native and foreign-born populations."*

Yet, despite a citizenship question being part of the census since the 13th Amendment was adopted in December 1865, when it was again included in the 2020 census survey, some members of Congress objected, and, on 14 March, Rep. Alexandria Ocasio-Cortez asked Commerce Secretary Wilbur Ross, *"While there's all of this debate about whether a citizenship question should be included or not included, the question I have is why are we violating the law to include any question whatsoever in the 2020 census?"*

Media reports on the hearing stated that there had been no citizen question after 1950, yet the 1960 census specifically asks where the person was born and the place of birth of both parents as well as the language spoken in the home (questions P8-P11). In the context of the questions, citizenship is implicit with American birth and alien status is implicit with foreign birth to foreign-born parents. Therefore, restoration of an explicit question serves to remove or clarify any implied status, and, combined with age, can yield an enumeration of eligible voters within each district. If one is planning to engage in voter fraud – stuffing the ballot box – the last thing you would want is a census indicating the maximum number of eligible voters in any given district.

Having raised the issue during the cycle period, at 9:30 AM on April Fools' Day, Trump tweeted, *"Can you believe that the Radical Left Democrats want to do our new and very important Census Report without the all important Citizenship Question. Report would be meaningless and a waste of the $Billions (ridiculous) that it costs to put together!"*

Ignoring the reality of the birthplace questions, an element among the Democrat asserted the citizenship question was going to discourage illegals from responding to the survey and therefore distort the data to reduce the number of Representatives allocated to the associated district. However, this makes little sense, since the current district count of 435 representatives, was fixed in law since 1911. The 1910 census indicated a population of 92 million and the 2010 census had 309.3 million – thereafter the population tripled without changing the Representative allocation. How large a distortion or undercount would be needed to effect a change that would reduce the 1911 standard?

The lack of change since 1911 introduces a ramifications problem that is reflected in complaints about the Electoral College being unrepresentative of the popular vote. But electoral votes are based on the number of representatives plus the two Senators for each State. But the number of Representatives has not changed in over a century, while the national population has tripled. The result is a proportional under-representation of the popular vote.

At a public forum in Mississippi, on 18 March, Elizabeth Warren declared, *"Every vote matters and the way we can make that happen is that we can have national voting, and that means get rid of the Electoral College."* But the Electoral College is not the problem. In 1911, the number of representatives was fixed at about one per 211 thousand people; in 2016, the population had grown to 323.4 million, making the ratio one to 743,5 thousand.

The Twelfth Amendment states, *"in choosing the President,*

the votes shall be taken by states, the representation from each state having one vote;" as should be clear, while increasing the number of Representatives would mean building a new Congress to house them – very costly. But a simple amendment to change the wording to add for words – *"the representation from each state having one vote for every 250,000 constituents"* – is all that is required to correct a population-based Electoral College problem. By advocating the elimination of the Electoral College, Warren *"throws out the baby with the bath-water."*

Now consider the Border Problem.

At the end of March, Homeland Security Secretary Kirstjen M. Nielsen stated that in February, *"we apprehended more than 75,000, the highest in over a decade. And now we are nearing 100,000 migrants per month."* Meaning the rate is approaching the annualized 1.6 million achieved in 2000.

According to the SUSPS, in 1972, the American fertility rate *"had voluntarily dropped to replacement level (2.1 children per woman)."* Since then, *population momentum* based on increased Baby-boomer longevity, and augmented by immigration, has been the driving force behind population growth.

This was confirmed by the SUSPS report, which stated the growth is keyed to two factors. The first is *"a period of time equal to the average life expectancy (approximately three generations ...) for a reduction in fertility to be manifested as a change in actual population numbers."* While the *"second, and much more significant reason is because of high levels of mass immigration into the United States."*

The 2001 report estimated that 65% of population growth *"will be the direct or indirect consequence of immigration."* The PEW Research Center, in 2015, reported the demographic trends indicated, as the population approaches mid-century levels of 441 million, 88% of that growth would be attributed to immigrants and their descendants.

At the time of the PEW projection, there were 329 million Americans and a growth rate of 2.3 million a year. The Southern border situation, as driven by Pelosi and Schumer, will increase that number by at least 50%, and, if nothing else, the states taking in these immigrants will lose their proportional voice in Congress.

As stated in 2001, *"Each year there are approximately 4 million births in the U.S. and 2.4 million deaths. The growth due to natural increase (total births minus deaths) is therefore 1.6 million per year. Yet according to the Census Bureau's decennial census, U.S. population is growing by approximately 3.3 million per year."* Latin Americans – lacking knowledge of English, with minimal education and skills being phased out or replaced by AI and automation – will be adding roughly an additional 1.6 million a year stress on depleting environmental resources such as fresh water.

We know *"unwanted births accounted for approximately 400,000 U.S. births per year in the mid-1990's."* We also know Right-wing Swamp Denizens are pushing to return to or exceed, those levels, while Senator Lee is on record promoting a general birthrate increase to ensure as much additional stress as possible is placed on depleting or limited environmental resources.

In his written 2001 testimony, Bill Elder used the example of a 13% census-to-census population increase on electric demand, which we can use to underscore Lee's anti-environment objectives.

Assuming the per capita consumption to be a constant, the increased population spawns a commensurate growth in demand; this means additional power plants fueled by natural gas and coal; which triggers a 2% increase in air pollution per megawatt, and a 15% increase in air pollution.

Of course, that scenario assumes the new demand is not met by environmentally friendly solar or wind power. In order for the 13% population grow to avoid additional harm to air quality, there would need to be a general reduction in power usage of 15%. And, while Elder testified at a time when illegal border crossing had yielded 1.6 million apprehensions, he did not account for that increase when discussing domestic birthrate effects, after writing, *"And then, do so again and again if Congress allows population growth to continue unabated in future decades."*

But first, Elder wrote: *"Taking a longer term view, the U.S. is the third most populated country in the world. With our de facto 'growth forever' population policy we are headed in the same direction as the first two - China and India. (The U.S. could hit a billion persons within about 100 years according to some*

Census Bureau scenarios.) We see the environmental damage these countries have experienced with only a fraction of the consumption per capita of the U.S. and find this vision of America very sobering."

He then warned of the events which have spawned Trumps Emergency Declaration – opposed by the *'growth forever'* faction of Congress – saying:

> *"The key is the Mexican Border. Climate change and social disruption of the economies to the south will cause mass migrations as large or larger than those currently being experienced. This will cause population growth that hampers work on climate control by undermining the American economy. Once the economy is damaged, America fall prey to aggressive nations. The benefit being, any war will see the immigrants of the right age for combat."*

Of course, we now have the Revelation timeline in *"Biblical Prophecy: Are we in the Revelation Era"* and can assert the war will be sometime in the mid-2030s, so the potential combat force will be composed of anyone born after 2005. Could it be possible the current anti-abortion movement is seeking cannon fodder – is that why Senator Lee wants to mass-produce babies ... to send them off to die? Some Republicans do favor anything that ensures *The Most Harm To The Most People.*

In terms of Trump's focus on the Border Wall, a 22 January 2019 article, in Scientific American, pointed to the connection between Global Warming and mass migration with an observation related to ramifications: *"Trump's rollback of carbon-fighting regulations could exacerbate mass migration in the Western Hemisphere and the world."*

We know that, just as The Great Wall of China stopped the Mongol from invading, ultimately, walls do not work. But they do deter some activities. However, to address the migration problem, we need to promote rapid growth in renewable Solar and Wind as compensation for individuals admitted into the country; this also addresses climate gases which, ultimately, will drive more people north. This would not negate the need for the border control and security the 2006 Secure Fence Act was to address.

CHAPTER NINE – RUSSIA 1956-2018

"We will either find a way or make one."
~ {allegedly} Hannibal
*"The only sure weapon against bad ideas
is better ideas."*
~ Alfred Whitney Griswold

Collusion, Conspiracy, Complicity, the exchange of money for information and propaganda; the things that are normal in any campaign or quest for power and are known to have been integral to the Clinton Campaign. Mueller, FaceBook and various Social Media platforms have clearly established that Russian information operatives focused their talents and efforts in those counties and election districts Clinton won by broad margins; yet, they appear noticeably absent in those districts where Trump won.

Of course, we had the Mueller investigation and the report released at the end of the second 57-week cycle, followed by Barr's letter inferring there was no collusion between Trump and Russia. But then, we heard that some of Robert S. Mueller's investigators had said Attorney General William P. Barr didn't properly portray the findings – he interpreted rather than quoted.

Throughout the Mueller investigation, the term everyone tossed about was "colluded" or "collusion", by in his four-page letter, Barr wrote "... *conspired with the Russian government in its efforts to interfere in the 2016 U.S. presidential election,...*" It is important to note 'collusion' is not a crime, but 'conspiracy' is – a point Barr makes explicit on page two of the letter.

Barr also told us that Mueller investigation was targeting *"attempts by a Russian organization, the Internet Research Agency (IRA), to conduct disinformation and social media operations in the United States designed to sow social discord, eventually with the aim of interfering with the election."* And, in that regard, charges bought against Russian nationals and others; none involving *"any U.S. person or Trump campaign official or associate..."*

In addition, it was found the computers and emails for both Clinton's campaign and the Democratic Party organizations were hacked and then released via WikiLeaks. But the nature of the hacking shows that concerns over Hillary's server were justified.

On April Fool's Day, Barr issued a follow-up memo stating: *"Special counsel Robert Mueller's report on his investigation into Russian election interference will be released publicly, with some redactions, by mid-April and possibly sooner."*

Barr's "summary" ceased being referred to as a "summary" – because it wasn't actually a summary, it was, as Barr phrased it, *"a summary of its 'principal conclusions' – that is, its bottom line.... I do not believe it would be in the public's interest for me to attempt to summarize the full report to release it in serial or piecemeal fashion."*

At this point in time, it would appear the actual Mueller Report will be released to Congress soon after publication of this addition to the *Trump Card Series*, what and when the public will see the report is a different matter. But, the issue we should all be concerned with is exactly who, if anyone, the Russians were trying to place in the Oval Office?

We know Russia hacked the Democrats, and that Clinton was presumed to be the odds-on favorite; we know Russian social media propaganda operations were concentrated in regions that went overwhelmingly to Clinton – but because social media is only dominant in a dozen extremely high population states, winning the popular vote does not translate into the votes necessary to win the Electoral College, and therefore does not 'win the election.'

Given the facts, there are a limited number of conclusions to be drawn from the Russian efforts: either they wanted Hillary to win, or were too incompetent to create propaganda of the type needed to sway opinion in the states and districts Clinton won. It is also clear that they could not manipulate the votes in smaller, more rural, States which tend to vote Republican and yielded the Electoral College votes needed for Trump's surprise victory.

As we know, Elizabeth Warren and others would like to end the Electoral College and thereby make it easier for the Russians or any other malevolent entity to manipulate the general election outcomes.

However, Russians think in terms of long-term goals. And in that context, we can look at data discovered by the MUCKROCK

FOIA news and information organization, which reported on CIA memos showing that the first record of Russian interference efforts involving U.S. elections date to the Kennedy era. The memos dated 1964 and 1982, establish Russian activities extended into the Reagan era; beyond that, the documents are not available through FOIA requests. However, as reported by Emma Best, on 19 July 2017, *"A formerly SECRET memo sent to the Director of Central Intelligence in 1982 reveals that the Intelligence Community's concern with Russian attempts to influence the U.S. Presidential election go back decades."*

Within the 28 October, 1982 memo is an assertion that the detected Soviet activities should be seen *"as part of a scheme to tip the 1984 U.S. elections."* The memo also states, *"after years of intense efforts...the Soviet grasp of the US political system is better than ever. Hence the Soviet capacity for influencing votes is higher."* That observation seems to negate any idea of Russians being unaware of the Electoral College.

To the contrary, they might actually have promoted Hillary with the objective of losing the Electoral College and initiating a move to eradicate it and thus make it easier for them to manipulate future "popular vote" based elections – ones in which only nine or ten states would be needed to achieve victory for their preferred candidate.

Technically, given that hypothesis, Russia had no reason to concern itself with a specific candidate or Party victory. They only needed to establish a foundation for their propaganda attacking the Electoral College. The report cites other sources who mention, *"during the Cold War, the Soviet Union used intelligence officers, influence agents, forgeries, and press placements to disparage candidates perceived as hostile to the Kremlin."*

Disparagement of Trump began almost immediately upon Trump's 16 June 2015 pronouncement, *"I am officially running for president of the United States, and we are going to make our country great again,"* the disparagement which defined the next three and a half years began. Given his style, the Russians did not need to attack the other candidates

As a salesman, Trump used what he knew had sold before, and basically plagiarized previous winners – from Reagan he took

"Make America Great Again"; while Obama and the Democrats gave him the 2006 Secure Fence Act and Schumer's 2013 Senate assertion of goals: *"Fewer illegal immigrants, higher GDP, more jobs, reduced deficits. Who could oppose that? I don't know of anybody ... if they care about America."* Then Donald tossed in the oft used idea of Draining the Swamp – used by Winfield R. Gaylord in 1903: *"Socialists are not satisfied with killing a few of the mosquitoes which come from the capitalist swamp; they want to drain the swamp."* And in 1912, Victor L. Berger wrote, *"We should have to drain the swamp – change the capitalist system..."*

It is curious that apparent origins of the expression came from men who were, like Bernie Sanders, Democratic Socialists in the days before there was a Russian Communist State. Of course, Ronald Reagan used the term to refer to the Federal bureaucracy, as has Nancy Pelosi. And looking at the expression, we see Trump had taken upon himself a bipartisan objective that is befitting of a general sales pitch to a yet to be defined audience.

What tactic and slogan had Hillary adopted?

We known she referred to residents of Republican States *"a basket of deplorables"*, and that she had a half-dozen egotistical slogans, none of them memorable – one, "Love Trumps Hate", may have had the effect of encouraging his Red State Voters to go side with Trump, to "Drain the Swamp" of professional politicians like Hillary, to build the Wall that Schumer had advocated, and thereby stopping the illegals who Obama had spoken against.

Trump was the egotist who placed his name on everything, and yet two Clinton slogans were *"Hillary For America"* and *"I'm With Her."* Neither of which offered a goal, at least not like those Trump had or Bernie Sanders' *"A Future To Believe In,"* which then gave rise to supporters saying *"Feel The Bern."*

Having apparently helped her win the popular vote, but the Electoral College system, denied them leverage over Hillary in the Oval – augmented by philandering hubby Bill as First Gentleman – thus the Russians lost any benefit they might have gained from a recipient of their op-research.

On page 164 of *"The Swamp Fights Back"* you can find this citation of Clinton connections to Russia:

"In 2010, the Russia firm Renaissance Capital, which is tied to Russian intelligence, paid Bill Clinton a half-million dollars for a speech in Moscow – which raises the question: Does Clinton speak Russian? Then there is the money Putin's confidant, Victor Kekselberg, and other Russian oligarchs have contributed to The Clinton Foundation. Plus, the Foundation received $2.35 million from Uranium One, which is owned by the Russians and controls 20% of the American uranium deposits – the purchase was a 2010 deal which required State Department approval, and, coincidently, Hillary was Secretary of State from 2009 to 2013."

One of the greatest tricks of any leader is the one utilized by the skilled hypnotist to guide his subject into a trance – you tell them to do what they are already doing; you tell them they will feel what they are already feeling. The subject then becomes aware of their own behavior, focuses upon it, and attributes to your power over them.

Nikita Khrushchev was doing this when he said:

"You Americans are so gullible.

No, you won't accept communism outright, but we'll keep feeding you small doses of socialism until you'll finally wake up and find you already have communism.

We won't have to fight you. We'll so weaken your economy until you'll fall like overripe fruit into our hands."

Americans, like every other human on the planet, are very gullible. That gullibility is the basis for Hans Christian Andersen short tale, THE EMPEROR'S NEW CLOTHES, first published in April 1837. It is a gullibility derived from a need to seek approval, to not be considered a fool and to travel with the herd – even as they stampede toward a cliff and behave in the manner attributed to Lemmings.

This Lemming Effect explains why movements begin very small and grow. Behavioral psychologists know, In order for the whole group to fall into a line of acceptance, you need to reach the critical mass point of 25% of a group agreeing.

That group can then go out and make their case in terms that focus on the preconceived ideas of the target audience they wish to convert to their cause. The Hypnotic trick of saying we are doing what you want so that what you want can be accomplished.

Khrushchev stated, *"we'll keep feeding you small doses of socialism."* Call it socialism and Americans are trained to rebel. But, call it Christianity, and quote the specific verses in the Bible which mandate the common care objective, and suddenly they are behaving in a Socialist manner. To rebel against that, many are seen to reject the Bible, yet, care for others is ingrained all species and so the Socialist programs grow under the guise of "common decency".

Khrushchev knew people could not escape the behavioral reality, even while he lied to his own people about delivering it to them. As he knew, and every competent hypnotist demonstrates, it is all in the phrasing.

Behaviorists and psychologists will tell you: *"You can get anyone to do anything if you phrase it properly."* People have no problem committing brutal murders if you tell them they are protecting their nation or their loved ones.

War is the ultimate form of murder. It can be fought for defensive or aggressive reasons. The ancient Scythian, a nomadic Eurasian people – whose military approach Russia used against Napoleon and Hitler's Nazi – believed in a defensive war based on an initially non-confrontational reaction to an invasive enemy. In terms of traditional animal "fight or flight" instinct, the Scythian would initially select flight. This would manifest in the immediate destruction of anything an invader might be able to use, while also retreating. The act of retreat draws the enemy in, the destruction denies them the ability to "live off the land" and so stretches their supply lines to the point where a small mobile force can disrupt them.

Americans used this tactic in the Revolutionary war; we all know of the French Resistance in the Second World War; we saw this in Vietnam and are now seeing it in Afghanistan. Now think of this in terms of Khrushchev's statement: *"We won't have to fight you. We'll so weaken your economy until you'll fall like overripe fruit into our hands."*

Russia would play the Scythian – an enemy which must be addressed but does not waste resources fighting you. In point of fact, their tactic was to do only enough to ensure their enemy would commit resources to a non-existent combat situation. For Russia, this meant focusing resources on systems that would force the United States to expand its military budget to ridiculous levels – in a manner that conferred no actual tactical military advantage.

The lack of tactical advantage has been repeatedly exposed, but not commented upon either in the legislature or the popular media. The exposure of the fundamental weakness, the goal that Khrushchev had realized was possible based on the Korean War, was seen again in Vietnam. Both Bush Administrations revealed that weakness to a world which stood witness to the operations called Desert Storm and the War on Terror. On October 7, 2001, the United States invaded Afghanistan, and that conflict was still in full force when Donald Trump took office on 20 January 2017.

When Obama took office, Bush had committed a hundred thousand troops, and we later learned some of them were based within line-of-sight of Osama Bin Laden's villa. When Obama can into Office, they did manage to find an kill Bin Laden, but Taliban forces remained undefeated.

Obama initiated a strategic shift from failed aggression to support services and by 2017, 90-percent of the military had been withdrawn. For fiscal year 2017, the Congressional Budget Office placed the US Military budget at 15-percent of the Federal Budget – an amount equal to $590 billion, or more than the combined budgets for the next seven highest nations combined.

Russia, which has more nuclear warheads than the United States, spends on $69.2 billion, which is 12% in dollar amounts, but in terms of GDP, is a third more. But, in terms of GDP, the US is number one, while Russia ranks twelfth. Comically the Russian bogeyman ranks fourth in military expenditures – behind Saudi Arabia and China [The People's Republic of China].

Khrushchev understood the US Military, like the French in Vietnam prior to the Second World War, or the Nazis during that war, was not equipped to fight a resistance or terrorist style war – and that played into his economic "passive destruction" strategy.

He also recognized another reality, the one the Scythian took advantage of. To exert an aggressive posture anywhere in the world, the United required a massive transportation and supply system which would prove extremely expensive in raw cost and the cost of diverted assets.

Thus, so long as America continues to waste money on the military, it remains on track to fulfill Khrushchev's objective. As we know, he also pointed toward the gradual rise of socialism in the United States, for which he only had to be aware of the history of the nation and Teddy Roosevelt advocating the creation of some form of National Health Care in 1912, and, in 1935, his cousin Franklin Delano Roosevelt created a government business called the Works Progress Administration (WPA) which focused on the construction and improvement of post offices, bridges, schools, highways, and parks, while being prohibited from competing with private industry. In the process, it also provided work for artists, writers, theater directors, and musicians.

The 1935 Social Security Act was an American version of a system established in Germany in 1889. Both were designed to be "pay-as-you-go" programs paid from current premiums paid in the form of a tax on payrolls, and both set the qualifying age at 65.

It is significant that life expectancy was less than 50-years old, while the population, therefore the expected revenue base, was growing at the rate of 34% per year. When Roosevelt initiated the program, the projected growth rate was 15% per year, Thus both nations had effectively instituted a tax people were happy to pay, but only had a 50% probability of collecting.

With the post-war baby-boom, which had peaked the year before Khrushchev first made his assertions, the demographics had changed, but the push for the social programs had not abated. People in Europe were accustomed to National Health and it was spreading. History decreed that America would follow their lead – but lag a half-century behind. Therefore, the point at which the opposition would need to be in power was around 1985, and, as we know from CIA documents dated 1982, they were convinced the Russians were playing to influence the 1984 election.

With Nixon's visit to China and his version of the 1899 US "Open Door Policy," he initiated the foundation for what would evolve into *"The New Silk Road"* or *"Belt and Road"* – the original "Silk Road" being credited to the Scythian merchants, whose combat technique Russia utilized against Napoleon and Hitler.

As quoted in *Khrushchev Remembers: The Last Testament* (1974):

"I remember President Kennedy once stated... that the United States had the nuclear missile capacity to wipe out the Soviet Union two times over, while the Soviet Union had enough atomic weapons to wipe out the United States only once... When journalists asked me to comment... I said jokingly, "Yes, I know what Kennedy claims, and he's quite right. But I'm not complaining... We're satisfied to be able to finish off the United States first time round. Once is quite enough. What good does it do to annihilate a country twice? We're not a bloodthirsty people."

Russia need not be bloodthirsty, they need only allow the American people to destroy themselves in the same way Adolph Hitler, in Mein Kampf, spoke of the Germans losing the first war by falling for foreign propaganda. To see the technique that Hitler claimed was used by Britain, look at the irrationality of the attacks on Trump. Those promoting impeachment are seeking to install Mike Pence into the Oval office, crash the Stock Market, and unify the voters behind the Republicans – because an economic disaster will be blamed on the Democrats.

Khrushchev's objectives were helped by Johnson, much the same way George W. Bush {Bush-43} helped Jihadists when he lied about WMD's, then using the American Military to murder Saddam Hussein, while the Saudis, whose people were responsible for 9/11, joined forces with the US and Britain to commit genocide in Yemen. Disrupting the Middle East opened the door to Russian entry into Syria. Then, when Venezuela imploded, Russia – who was already their oil money banker – started to move in, knowing the US Congress was opposing all things Trump Latin America.

When Lyndon Baines Johnson ascended to the Oval Office after the assassination of John Fitzgerald Kennedy, America found itself with a 'hawk' in the Oval Office. Fifty years later, in the Bush era, LBJ represented Right-Wing Republican perfection – one advocating, in 1964, a variation of the 'Domino Theory':

"If we quit Vietnam tomorrow we'll be fighting in Hawaii and next week we'll have to be fighting in San Francisco."

That was Bush screaming about Hussein and nonexistent

Weapons of Mass Destruction {WMD's}. Hussein was fighting the sectarian imperialism which has defined Islam for 1400 years and had worked with Reagan against Iran. But Bush-43 was partners with the Saudis and Bin Laden family, and they wanted Hussein gone. Everyone seems to want someone gone.

For over a generation, the Vietnamese had been fighting for their freedom from French Colonialism, they had no interest in being a Russian Colony, and certainly no interest in attacking America. They simply wanted to be the country they are – the one America had promised them during World War Two.

A willingness to fight wars facilitating manipulation of the internal affairs of other nations has become a political touchstone that defines the ideal Republican. Of course, we have seen Trump attacked for having 'bone spurs', but that is a weak attack among voters who fought against Vietnam, and meaningless to those too young to remember a life defined by the idea that Selective Service could send you to your death because a sovereign people decided they didn't want your country to dictate their form of government.

Beginning with Lyndon Johnson Vietnam began to add to the growth in the National Debt, which went from an inflation consistent 3% to 13%; then, under Nixon it grew by 34%; Ford added another 47%; Carter, who had to deal with the Oil Embargo and Iran Hostage crisis, added another 43% and that was the last time the National Debt was below the trillion dollar mark.

In December 1998, the House of Representative initiated the impeachment of Bill Clinton, who, the previous year had only had a $22 billion deficit, which ended a four year period in which the total deficit was $496 billion. Clinton's crime hinged on the fact he defined "sexual relations" as requiring "intercourse" and thus being the illicit activity his accuser, Newt Gingrich repeatedly engaged in when committing adultery with younger women. All Clinton had done was enjoy a bit of satisfying "Oral in the Oval".

Clinton's real crime was, he consistently showed a budget surplus when the goal was to plunge America into debt. Gingrich, being typical of Right-wing Republicans, would have preferred a Ronald Reagan whose $1.412 trillion increased the National Debt by 142%; then George H. W. Bush, added another $1.036 trillion deficit in his four years. Later George Junior would add $5.849

trillion, to increase the National Debt by 101%, while triggering the Great Recession that forced Barack Obama to add yet another $8.599 Trillion and add 74% to the Republican-generated Debt Burden.

These numbers and percentages reflect first-year amounts as belonging to the prior administration that passed the budget; they are considerably different if they are calculated based simply on the calendar dates of each POTUS term. Still, it was a pattern begun with Reagan's Voodoo Economics that has caused potential problems which the nation's enemies seek to capitalize on.

Of course, there is a move to impeach Trump, whose four-year projected budgets would only increase the Debt by 29% – or only $4.775 Trillion in his first four-year term. Since Clinton was working against the Reagan-Bush policies, despite his surplus, Clinton had still managed to increase the National Debt by 32%. Still, the final four fiscal years under Clinton returned sufficient surpluses to yield an eight-year surplus of $63 billion, ultimately reducing the National Debt by one percent.

There is a comparative problem arising from the fact that much of the National Debt is money the nation owes itself. Or, as chief Capital Economics economist Paul Ashworth phrased it, "*It's a little misleading because that is the gross amount, which includes 'debt' that various federal government departments owe to other departments. ... In particular, it includes nonmarketable debt that the federal government 'owes' to the social security and Medicare funds.*"

There is no question the government spends more than it takes in. But, when the Baby-Boomers die – which will effectively be around 2040 – all the debt associated with their benefits will evaporate.

In 1956, when Khrushchev threatened America would be destroyed from inside, through its own actions, the Budget was also returning a nearly one percent surplus.

Coincidently, Russia fell into a financial crisis on 17 August 1998; as a result, the ruble was devalued, and the nation defaulted on its domestic debt while declaring a moratorium on repayment of foreign debt. Russia was in serious trouble. The kind of trouble the Republicans had begun to push upon America in a manner that Clinton had brought an end to.

Could Russia tolerate America having a POTUS who put an end to the trouble that now was consuming it?

On 25 July 1998, Vladimir Vladimirovich Putin, then 45-years-old, became Director of the Federal Security Service; less than 9-months later, he was Secretary of the Security Council; 5-months after that, First Deputy Prime Minister of Russia; then, 9-years after that, on 7 May 2008, he was running the government.

It's interesting that, by the 2000 election which pitted Bush against Gore, coincided with Putin moving beyond any position involving Security, espionage, or propaganda, and suddenly a major election was reduced to a dispute involving hanging chads in one Florida county. Still, with the Republican victory, we saw the destruction of the World Trade Center by terrorists with valid visa documents and a two-term $3.293 trillion deficit.

CHAPTER TEN – MUELLER

"This is collusion illusion, there is no smoking gun here. At this late date, …, we have no Russian Collusion. There is nothing impeachable here."
~ **@realDonaldTrump 11:01 AM - 8 Dec 2018**

Allegedly, the purpose of the Mueller investigation was to explore the facts related to any Russian interference with the 2016 election. As we know from the Khrushchev statement of 1956, and CIA memo of 1964, which can be said to support his statement of 1963, there is ample history to assert an ongoing pattern of interference that Mueller should incorporate into any report. In December 2018, evidence of that came to light with an AP based HuffPost report stating:

> *"Russia's sweeping political disinformation campaign on U.S. social media was more far-reaching than originally thought, with troll farms working to discourage black voters and "blur the lines between reality and fiction" to help elect Donald Trump in 2016, according to reports released Monday by the Senate intelligence committee."*

Did Russia really want Trump to win? Their focus on social media only impacted Hillary Clinton territory and resulted in her overwhelming dominance in the popular vote – indicating Russia failed. Trolls had no means of affecting the Electoral College; any effort to target 'black voters' would have had to focus on regions with a high black population – areas where gerrymandering was already swaying the vote to the Republicans.

While the focus on the Clinton-Trump results could be a matter of importance, the real interference based on the nature of the American government, what occurs in the Halls of Congress. Congress follows a long-term pattern one involving the election of individuals who are there for decades.

A quick Google search revealed a Wikipedia page listing the members of Congress based on longevity, and revealed that there were/are 100 House and 55 Senate members, who served between 36 to 56 years.

In terms of election-influencing, the problem Mueller faces

is one of rationality. If an intelligent enemy wants to influence another government, unless that government is a dictatorship, it is the Congress or Parliament that they would want to control or disrupt. Has the Congress been influenced to the point where its members attack the traditional policies and beliefs which got them elected?

What this reveals is, if one wanted to disrupt the nation, the goal would be to place moles in the respective houses of Congress, and work the propaganda to ensure them the longevity needed to slowly and methodically modify legislation in a way that would create the maximum damage to the nation – such as ensuring a budget would run a deficit and increase the National Debt to the point where an inability to pay would cause a Constitutional crisis, one reflective of the economic problem Russia itself experienced in 1998.

With both Trump and Hillary, we see results that reflect the same "straight ticket" voting patterns that are consistent with the states they won. To some extent, we can say the election outcome was determined by those eligible voters who stayed home.

The media has chosen to set its focus on a meeting which occurred at Trump Tower, on 9 June 2016, and invoke the term "Collusion" as if it involved a "Criminal Conspiracy," when there is no dispute over the fact it was standard "Opposition Research."

Here is the inherent problem of conflating collusion with conspiracy is that, while collusion can be an illegal conspiracy, it can be used when working together toward a common goal. Thus, the issue is one of the specifics. If any entity indicates it supports a candidate, it is, of necessity, colluding with that candidate. It is true that collusion is also defined in terms of secret cooperation or conspiracy designed to cheat or deceive others, and it can be the *"illegal cooperation or conspiracy, especially between ostensible opponents in a lawsuit."*

Suppressing information about a legal personal activity is not something that cheats or deceives unless it is held that tabloid quality news must be made public – negating the idea of "invasion of privacy." Is a Non-Disclosure Agreement payment a campaign contribution? How about the purchasing of the right to the story, explicitly for the purpose of not publishing, but, instead to keep it from being published? How about "donations" or non-candidate approved advertising which promotes or attacks the candidates' agenda?

It is said that *"With any conspiracy charge, the crime is the agreement itself."* It is because of this legal based definition that the media avoids the term "conspiracy" – to use it becomes an explicit assertion of criminal behavior, and invokes the rules of evidence and a basis for a lawsuit charging slander.

As former the New York Prosecutor and Trump attorney, Rudolph W. Giuliani, stated, *"I have been sitting here looking in the federal code trying to find collusion as a crime. Collusion is not a crime."*

As pointed out in THE WASHINGTON POST article on the topic, *"What matters in criminal law is the facts, not the precise terms used to describe what happened."* This means that simply meeting with people who claim to fact background data on an opponent is a crime – or will be if there is an indictment that does not detail a real and commonly recognized crime.

The POST references 923. 18 U.S.C. § 371 – Conspiracy to Defraud the United States, which states, if *"two or more persons conspire either to commit any offense against the United States, or to defraud the United States, or any agency thereof in any manner or for any purpose."*

Applying this statute would seem to make the election of a candidate an *"offense against the United States"*. Conversely, based on the reasons and justifications for Op-Research, it also makes it an un-prosecuted crime to oppose a candidate. Certainly, Hillary Clinton having paid Russian for op-research, and having received campaign or other money from Russians, should trigger an investigation every bit as detailed as Mueller's had been. There is the issue of the "Steele Dossier" – the Russia-Trump connection invented by former British MI6 officer Christopher Steele –which were commissioned by Hillary Clinton's campaign via Fusion GPS.

Of course, so long as Hillary stays away from politics, any investigation would be a waste of taxpayer money. But her actions or those of her campaign would seem to meet a definition applied to a law dealing with a conspiracy *"for the purpose of impairing, obstructing or defeating the lawful function of any department of government...*"

Of course, it would not apply to anything which is intended to provide voters with the information to ensure an informed vote.

Trump affirmed that "Opposition Research" is a common practice when he Tweeted the purpose was, "*to get information on an opponent, totally legal and done all the time in politics – and it went nowhere. I did not know about it!*"

Whether or not Trump had any awareness of the meeting beforehand actually isn't relevant. The relevant issue is one of the legalities of engaging in the gathering of data relative to a political opponent. If such behavior is deemed illegal, then every member of Congress has committed criminal activities or has explicitly hired someone to engage in criminal activity. If it is legal, then it is legal – and only the act of hiring someone to invent or falsify information would be illegal.

It clearly benefits Russian Trolls and the tabloid media to promote Opposition Research being the basis for things consistent with "Collusion" or criminal conspiracy. If carried to its logical conclusion, this invokes the potential for a Constitutional crisis. It should be noted that the function of a PAC – Political Action Committee – is to "Collude" with a candidate in a manner which allows circumvention of Campaign Finance Laws.

In the context of the Trump Tower meeting, Trump lawyer Jay Sekulow has been quoted saying, "*The question is how would it be illegal?*" He went on to say, ask, and state, "*The question is, what law, statute or rule or regulation has been violated? No one has pointed to one.*"

Clearly, there was no effort to conceal a meeting that was a matter of public record prior to the election. We also know that, as early as August 2016, US Intelligence agencies had determined they had grounds to believe the emails published by Wikileaks had been stolen by Russian hackers or spies.

Once those emails were in the public area, Trump had every legal right to refer to them, and, in that context, correctly asserted there was no way to determine who the actual thief had been.

However, this proved costly Stormy Daniels', when Michael Avenatti, her attorney, tried to achieve Non-Disclosure Agreement nullification by publically promoting the information that was the subject of the NDA he had brought a lawsuit to nullified.

In the last week of August 2018, *The Daily Caller* web site published an exclusive report which grabbed Trump's attention, and quite naturally resulted in a Tweet: *"Report just out: "China hacked Hillary Clinton's private Email Server." Are they sure it wasn't Russia (just kidding!)? What are the odds that the FBI and DOJ are right on top of this? Actually, a very big story. Much classified information!"*

Quoting a comment by Texas Republican Representative Louie Gohmert, made during a hearing with former FBI agent Peter Strzok, the article stated: *"The Intelligence Community Inspector General (ICIG) found an 'anomaly on Hillary Clinton's emails going through their private server, and when they had done the forensic analysis, they found that her emails, every single one except four, over 30,000, were going to an address that was not on the distribution list.... going to an unauthorized source that was a foreign entity unrelated to Russia'"*

Apparently, when the server was examined by the FBI, they failed to notice the emails were clearly labeled "(C)" indicating the document was classified and being sent to an instant "Courtesy Copy" – meaning the transfer occurred in real-time conjunction with all the authorized transmissions. It wasn't a hack so much as a realtime standard backup or cloud update which could escape detection by anti-spyware software.

We also learned that, on 21 July 2015, former FBI Deputy Director Mark F. Giuliano sent a follow-up memo to President Obama which said: *"On 13 July 2015 and 20 July 2015, I verbally advised you of a Section 811(c) referral from the Inspector General of the Intelligence Community received by the FBI on 06 July 2015. The referral addressed the mishandling of classified information on the personal e-mail account and electronic media of a former high-level us Government official."*

So, apparently, there is documentation that Obama knew Clinton's server had been hacked, and classified data provided to foreign actors. In other quoted statements and documents we are informed *"there's evidence based on the complete lack of security hygiene on the server. Fourteen-year-old hackers from Canada could have probably hacked into her server and left very little trace. there's evidence based on the complete lack of security hygiene on the server. Fourteen-year-old hackers from Canada could have probably hacked into her server and left very little trace "*

It would appear Trump was vindicated. Not through any justification for the "Crooked Hillary" slogan, but clearly through the call to focus on the 30,000 emails which were deleted and we were now learning included classified back copied to China. Then there is the apparent fact that the FBI experts who have since left or been fired missed it when they did their security check of the system – and Obama knew about it.

Trump also yells about "FakeNews", and those attacking Trump have asserted the Tweet about China is just a distraction from real issues. So, which is the "FakeNews", the documentation or the media assertion? China responded to the revelation in the same way Russia did, only they focused on Trump, with the State newspaper pointing out what was being said in the States: *"Since his supporters have shown a willingness to suspend disbelief, we can no doubt look forward to more such tales."* And turning to the distraction technique, the added, *"smearing China's image as he desperately needs a scapegoat in the run-up to the midterm elections, so he can divert public attention from the troubles the White House has become mired in."*

What will Mueller focus on? Will he give China a free pass like the one Bush gave to Bin Laden?

Prior to Mueller, Trump fired FBI director James Comey, who, just days before the election, violated protocol and issued a letter in which he inferred there was new evidence for a renewed email related criminal investigation of Clinton. Obviously, Comey had intentionally acted to sway the election by formally providing the appearance of a basis for the Trump campaign chant, "LOCK HER UP."

Mueller came in to take over the Russia investigation,

On Friday, December 7, 2018, Comey was interviewed by the House Committee on the Judiciary, and related his view on the Russian Investigation with the words: *"To my mind, the term 'Russia investigation' often refers to two different things: First, the investigation to understand what are the Russians doing to interfere in our election during the 2015-16 period; and then, second, it's often used to refer to the counterintelligence investigations that the FBI opened in late July."*

Representative Harold Watson "Trey" Gowdy then said: *"Okay. We'll go with that. Late July of 2016, the FBI did, in fact, open a counterintelligence investigation into, is it fair to say the Trump campaign or Donald Trump himself?"*

Comey then corrected him: *"It's not fair to say either of those things, in my recollection. We opened investigations on four Americans to see if there was any connection between those four Americans and the Russian interference effort. And those four Americans did not include the candidate."*

Representative John Ratcliffe would later shift the focus to Hillary Clinton and the decision not to prosecute Hillary Clinton for the mishandling of classified information. The banter made it clear that there could be have been grounds, and nothing has changed, saying: *"There was material that had not been verified that I believed if it became public would be used to cast doubt on whether the Attorney General had acted appropriately with respect to the investigation. I haven't gone -- I don't think I'm allowed to go beyond that in characterizing that material."*

Ratcliffe clarified the lengthy exchange with the question: *"So I guess as I try and summarize what I've heard today, Hillary Clinton mishandled classified information more than a hundred times. She made false statements about it. The FBI was aware that at least one of her aides also mishandled classified information. And one of the folks employed on behalf of Secretary Clinton intentionally destroyed evidence known to be subject to a congressional subpoena and preservation order and lied to the FBI about it. And on July 5th, 2016, you stood before the American people and said that neither you nor any reasonable prosecutor would bring any charges in this fact pattern. Is that accurate?"*

Comey responded: *"Yep. I believed it then, I believe it now. And anybody that thinks we were on team Clinton trying to cut her a break is smoking something."*

And with that response, Comey established both the intent behind his breach of protocol and the high probability that there would have been valid charges leveled against a President Hillary Clinton. Those charges carrying the added problem that they would underscore the idea that Hillary could not be trusted with the *classified information* which, of necessity, is in the hands of a President.

Looking at Mueller's investigation, by 5 August 2018 three Russian companies and thirty-two individuals, including lobbyist, political consultant, and attorney Paul J. Manafort Jr., who had served as Trump's deputy campaign chairman were all indicted with multiple guilty pleas negotiated – of those, five individuals had plead guilty to crimes not related to the election, and the charges against Manafort focused on a previous instance of tax and bank fraud.

The case against Manafort apparently hinged on testimony from political consultant Richard W. Gates III, who had been indicted along with Manafort, then entered into a plea bargain agreement to avoid further criminal charges.

The charges against Manafort revolved around money he received or controlled while serving as an advisor in presidential campaigns of Republicans Gerald Ford, Ronald Reagan, George H. W. Bush, and Robert J Dole, who was defeated by Bill Clinton.

The trial, where only the prosecution provided any witness testimony; in his closing arguments, Manafort attorney Richard Westling pointed out that banks had not informed regulators of any problems or irregularities with the Manafort accounts. It was when "the special counsel came and asked questions," that the account information became relevant, indicating the prosecutors were "stacking" charges against Manafort.

In rebuttal, the prosecutors asserted the defense was in violation of an agreement no to politicize case, and, in his jury instructions, Senior United States District Judge Thomas Selby Ellis directed the jury to ignore suggestions the prosecution was politically motivated. Jury deliberation began on 15 August; they reported they verdict six days later – guilty on 8 counts of bank and tax fraud, with a mistrial declared on ten additional counts.

With the verdict came news that attorney Michael Cohen pled guilty eight charges in an unrelated case. Cohen also made the extraordinary admission of having paid pornographic actress

Stormy Daniels, "at the direction of the candidate," in connection with a non-disclosure agreement related to an affair she said they had in 2006. Trump had become the Republican candidate on 26 May 2016, Stormy then came forward with her threat to go public, unless she was paid to keep quiet, and the agreement was dated 28 October 2016.

Among the charges Cohen pled guilty to was an allegation that the payments violated campaign finance laws. Cohen also admitted to unrelated charges he lied to avoid paying taxes and to banks in order to obtain improper loans. But, the issue remains, is the use of personal funds, to pay off a blackmailer, a violation of Campaign Funding Law?

Apparently, two unnamed women were also paid for their silence. But this relates to avoidance of tabloid type media stories which could have influenced the electorate in the same way the Comey letter seemed to have affirmed the "Crooked Hillary" rhetoric. Curiously, it was a threat to influence the election would have been behind Daniel's approaching Trump, so, in effect, was she "blackmailing" the Trump on two levels – one being Trump's position as both *"Apprentice"* Producer and Star, the other being that of POTUS candidate. In that context, Daniels might well have violated the law; she did violate the agreement by publicizing her filing of a lawsuit to nullify it – she disclosed the information the agreement said was not to be disclosed.

However, it was rather telling that tabloid media logic held that Trump was guilty because Cohen made a deal to plead guilty, but that what he pled guilty to did not apply to the related action by FBI Director James Comey.

While Cohen's plea bargain agreement had no provision for future cooperation, it did open the door to the interesting legal problem – does a Non-Disclosure Agreement constitute a form of illegal election manipulation in the context of Comey's letter, which inferred candidate Clinton was under criminal investigation and, if elected, could be indicted prior to taking the Oath of Office?

With the plea agreement, prosecutors effectively achieve a classification of a candidate sponsored NDA as a crime, which had the effect of making Trump a co-conspirator. But the suppression of a 'gossip' based tabloid news story would need to be a criminal act, either 'by definition' or in the context of a political campaign.

However, it must be recognized that no court has ever ruled it illegal to keep extramarital affairs secret. There is also an issue of whether a candidate is legally obligated to reveal information about themselves or their opponent – if so, does that obligation extents to the nature of their sex-life going back a decade or more before they became a candidate?

In a legal context, the argument hinges upon what can be called the public's right to know. In that context, it could be claimed that this touches "Freedom of the Press" and the right of David Pecker, CEO American Media Inc – the parent company of National Enquirer – to purchase exclusive rights to a story for the purpose of "killing" or concealing it from the public.

Does anyone have a right NOT to make public any and all facts concerning their life or the lives of others? The "interfering with an election" argument being used to attack was premised on the idea that no such right exists – all public or private individuals must reveal all aspects their private life so that it can be reported by the media, whenever the individual is deemed "newsworthy."

And, when reporting on an individual, all those facts must be made public. In the case of David Pecker, he followed what is known as a "*catch and kill*" deal policy whereby a publisher will acquire the exclusive rights to a story and then, as a personal or professional favor, or distort the story, doesn't publish what it has bought the exclusive rights to.

When, as Pecker routinely did, information that is deemed potentially detrimental to a political campaign is suppressed, it is clearly – based on the Cohen plea – a long-term ongoing criminal activity. It could even be a criminal conspiracy involving everyone in the publishing organization who had knowledge of it.

Obviously, we also have a fundamental Campaign Finance Law requirement Catch-22 involving suppression of potentially detrimental information which involves the public's right to know and an individual's right to privacy. It also involves Freedom of the Press and a definition of what is actually meant to constitute a "Campaign Contribution". When American Media Inc buys a story and then buries it to prevent the effect it would have on an election, aren't they interfering with the election?

Alan Dershowitz, Harvard Law School Emeritus professor of law, saw nothing illegal associated with the Cohen-Daniels NDA Dershowitz pointed out that Supreme Court Justice Scalia, who died in 2016, had said he couldn't figure out what campaign laws cover and do not cover, only that campaign funds must be used for legitimate campaign expenditures rather than personal ones. If the NDA is personal, then it is not campaign-related and therefore not a violation of the Campaign Finance Laws.

This raises the issue of whether Businessman Trump would have secured an NDA; as had been well publicized, NDA's are a normal business practice for Trump and the Trump Organization. It, therefore, falls on any prosecutor to prove in absolute terms that the money paid came from dedicated Campaign accounts and not from any of the vast resources of the Trump Organization.

The annual salary for a member of Congress is $174,000; prior to 2012, the Membership initiation fee at Trump's Mar-a-Lago Golf Club was $200,000; Stormy received a payment of only $130,000 in exchange for signing the NDA – which is less than the after-tax value of one new Mar-a-Lago membership.

Assuming Trump's business generates basic after-tax cash flow, the money paid to Stormy is insignificant, so why would Trump need to use campaign funds? This is complicated by the fact that a candidate is free to loan or advance funds to a campaign and then be repaid. So to argue illegal use of campaign funds is to argue no money was advanced by Trump – if we assume the check which paid Stormy was drawn on a designated campaign account.

We can contrast the threats of charges against Trump with the 60 count indictment brought against California Congressman Rep. Duncan Hunter and his wife Margaret Hunter, who used the funds for items that are objectively personal and have no rational connection to campaign-related expenses.

NEWSWEEK stated these included "*dental work, holidays, golf days, racetrack outings, theater tickets, family groceries, school fees, fast food, clothing, consumer electronics, alcoholic drinks and more—all despite warnings and queries by the campaign treasurer.*"

Concurrent with the Cohen plea, at least thirteen law school professors, scholars who specialize in these matters, opened the door to court actions which would result in creating an interesting legal prescient regarding opposition research and the possibility that the Finance Laws actually require candidates to provide any and all information detriment to their campaign to the opposition candidate.

In effect, all candidates would need to disclose details of their sex lives and personal contacts – as well as details of source and use of all money handled by anyone associated with them or their campaign. Any failure to do so would be a criminal act.

Prior to and subsequent to the Cohen guilty plea deal, there was talk of Trump issuing a pardon. On 22 August, Lanny Davis, Cohen's lawyer, told NPR:

"I know that Mr. Cohen would never accept a pardon from a man that he considers to be both corrupt and a dangerous person in the oval office. And he has flatly authorized me to say under no circumstances would he accept a pardon from Mr. Trump."

Of course, this "I'll take my punishment" statement came in conjunction with the announcement that Cohen had established a GoFundMe page entitled "Truth Fund," which was seeking about a half million dollars intended *"to help Michael Cohen and his family as he goes forward on his journey, to tell the truth about Donald Trump."*

Clearly, by accepting a pardon Cohen would undermine his ability to profit from his conviction by joining those who allege to be revealing insider truths. In his court statement, Cohen was careful not to explicitly identify Trump, instead, Cohen played a lawyer's inference game and said *"a federal candidate for office."*

The same deflection technique was used by Davis when he denied his client would ever *"accept a pardon from a man that he considers to be both corrupt and a dangerous person in the Oval Office."* The deflection is to attack Trump, and thus establish for potential publishers that Cohen might author a best selling attack book like Newman's *"Unhinged."*

"The question is how would it be illegal?" Sekulow said. *"The question is, what law, statute or rule or regulation has been violated? No one has pointed to one."* While there is no law, the argument that an NDA payment is a campaign contribution gets

interesting when it is asserted the information would influence the election. If publishing or not publishing something is deemed to outside "Freedom of the Press" – which would be the freedom *not* to report, or to report, information unfavorable to a candidate, then it would follow that publishing a book which is derogatory to a candidate is a contribution to their opponent.

This would mean the various books which attack Trump are therefore campaign contributions to the Democratic Party which must be reported. If they are not, it becomes a clear violation of the campaign finance laws. Now, obviously the books can be published, but only after the person who is the topic is no longer a political candidate or factor in current politics. Potentially, this is a Constitutional matter, but everything about "collusion" based on a standard practice NDA should be outside of Mueller's area of investigation – unless the Russian money paid for the NDA.

In 2017, a Russia related comment by British Conservative MP John Naughton, *"What is at stake is whether Russia has constructed an architecture which means they have thousands of accounts with which they can bombard [us] with fake news and hyper-partisan content. We need to understand how widespread it is and what the impact is on the democratic process."*

In 2018, Naughton's comment has been confirmed by the social media giants announcing they had identified and blocked the more obvious Russian Trolls or propagandists. The process of identifying Trolls who changed tactics had also begun.

As the evidence mounted, it became clear that the same actors were involved in both the 23 June 2016 British BREXIT referendum and 8 November 2016 American Presidential election.

The Trolls were smart, in conjunction with or immediately after, the referendum, they began the process of changing the public's focus, with tweets like, *"I hope UK after #BrexitVote will start to clean their land from Muslim invasion!"* and *"UK voted to leave future European Caliphate! #BrexitVote."*

Anti-Muslim racism in Britain is driving the movement to economic its economic problems. Looking back to the 1930s, it has been shown – in *Jonathon's POTUS COUSINS* – that British bigotry, antisemitism, and nationalism helped created the Second World War. It now seems that 'belligerent actors' have again seen fit to utilize and capitalized upon Britain's hatred for "The Other" and their need to dominate Europe, even at the cost of their own economic downfall.

So it is that, with a Mueller Report submitted, and Attorney General Barr having written a 'summary' that indicates Trump has been exonerated based on any and all evidence crimes which lead to the indictments and convictions spawned by Mueller's team, it falls upon those who seek to bring down the United States to find other avenues to pursue.

Those avenues will begin to be defined as the third 57-week period ends with the Russian May Day celebration, 1 May 2020; the next 56-week cycle ends 10 April 2020, and so we will have a 21-day period in which to anticipate all kinds of initial pre-convention posturing in final preparation for a 13-16 July 2020 Democratic Convention, to be followed five-weeks later with the Republican Convention on 24-27 August 2020.

Having apparently failed to undermine the government via Mueller, the Swamp Denizens have reverted to a focus on Trump's Tax Returns. For the first time since the 1974 changes in the laws governing Tax returns, the House Ways and Means Committee is seeking to investigate records normally only looked at when there is evidence of fraud in taxpayer current returns.

In the meantime, the request for tax records coincided with a Jobs report – 172,000 were anticipated, the actual was 196,000 'created' in March. Not only did the numbers comfortably exceed market projections, they marked the next step in what had become the longest streak of consecutive jobs growth on record. Reality did peak through, as unemployment held at 3.8 percent, with the average wage at $27.70 per hour with an average 34.5 hour work week.

Of course, post-Mueller investigation report actions clearly affirm that American represents an environment where there is a political climate defined by Impeachment seeking a justification. At the same time, border facilities have reached capacity and there was every indication that Congress desired only to ignore reality – both of the immediate problems, and those which will follow the realities of Climate Change.

CHAPTER ELEVEN - WALLS & FENCES

"We simply cannot allow people to pour into the United States undetected, undocumented, unchecked and circumventing the line of people who are waiting patiently, diligently and lawfully to become immigrants into this country." ~ **Senator Barack Obama, 2005**

In 2005, then-Senator Obama stated there were 11 million undocumented illegals in the country, the following year, he was among those voting for the 2006 Secure Fence Act that funded the first 700 miles of a border fence to be completed under President Obama.

In 2006, Presidential Candidate Obama told his campaign manager, David Plouffe: "I think I could probably do every job on the campaign better than the people I'll hire to do it." Of course, in 2019, when Donald Trump exhibits the same self-confidence as Obama, he is attacked – he is attacked for being a leader.

Leadership is a characteristic motivating mediocre failures to seek the removal of the leader. They can be 'Birthers' and seek to invalidate the individual's right to hold the position, or they can pursue a quest for anything that might be spun into a justification for impeachment. The game was played with Clinton, Obama, and is now being played with Trump. Had it been Hillary Clinton who won the Electoral College vote, she would be the target subject or game-goal.

None of that alters the reality that immigration is one of the more important problems in an age of Climate Change and social unrest. Immigration is also the transitional issue which marks the current shift between cyclical periods – in this case, the end of the first 57 election cycles and the beginning of what may, if America survives, define the next 228-years of history. For Evangelicals, it is the last phase in the "End of Times" prophecy culminating in a Third World War that happens sometime around 2033/35 and involves Middle Eastern nations attacking the Eurozone.

Bernie Sanders made it very clear he was having none of it. He wasn't buying the open border goal being pushed by Pelosi and Schumer. And, on 8 April, he said as much when he refuted a reporter's assertion he was onboard with the Democratic leaders: *"I'm afraid you may be getting your information wrong. I think what we need is comprehensive immigration reform. Oh my god, there's a lot of poverty in this world, and you're going to have people from all over the world. And I don't think that's something that we can do at this point. Can't do it."*

As Bernie was expressing his position, one which, in real terms, is in line with Trump's, he was also being declared the front runner in the race for the 2020 Democratic nomination. Now that Bernie seems to have affirmed his support for Secure Fence Act of 2006 – which, contrary to the Reagan Republican mindset, began as House legislation submitted by Republican Congressman Peter King of New York.

The Fence was and should remain, bipartisan. When the legislation was signed, Bush-43 said: *"This bill will help protect the American people. This bill will make our borders more secure. It is an important step toward immigration reform."*

At the time, it was opposed by Pelosi, and she continued to oppose it – promoting insecure borders while opposing rational immigration policies, are Hallmarks of the California Reaganite political mindset. But, before there was the 9-11 need for the law, immigration reform was a Democratic objective and, in August 2016, Trump expressed a type of praise for Obama's immigration enforcement efforts that he is criticized for when he directs it at the leaders of various nations.

Back then, Candidate Trump told Fox News: *"What people don't know is that Obama got tremendous numbers of people out of the country. Bush, the same thing. Lots of people were brought out of the country with the existing laws. Well, I'm going to do the same thing."*

Of course, the second 57-week cycle was defined by trump being attacked for taking a more modest approach to the border problem than the extreme one Obama was praised for. Every year of his administration, Obama's Department of Homeland Security booted out more illegals than Bush-43, who had ousted more than Clinton. In 2012 alone, Obama removed over 400,000 people.

The increased expulsions began with the authority granted by passage of the 1996 Illegal Immigration Reform and Immigrant

Responsibility Act. As the levels of enforcement increased, the number of adults entering the country illegally decreased and that caused deportations to decrease to 235,413 in fiscal year 2015.

The first months of 2019, saw an increased level of illegal entries which reflected the rhetoric of the anti-Trump, pro-Open Borders, group championed by Pelosi and Schumer – where it had been adults seeking work off-the-books, it became children and families with children with no capability of working. Roughly two-thirds of those crossing the border were children many of whom were intentionally unaccompanied, so there would be no question of them being confined to detention centers under some false guise of "*family reunification*."

Foreign nationals know that "*family reunification*" was the excuse to confine children in temporary enclosures that could be labeled or depicted as "*cages*" by those who have no concern for either the asylum seekers or the nation – they just want variations of political optics to further perpetual attacks of the government.

The 2006 Secure Fence Act had produced structures which Trump characterized as a "Wall." The "Fence" – the barbed wire and steel planks – which had been built had proved too weak and within a decade of construction required extensive improvement and repair.

To obfuscate matters, the Trolls attacked the idea of a Wall, while being careful to avoid reference to the reality that, had been a matter of legislative law for a dozen years. In effect, they were taking advantage of Trump's habit of plagiarizing any sales pitch which had been proven to work – such as Reagan's *Make America Great Again.*

In 1980, Reagan had opposed the "Fence" and promoted an Amnesty; once in office, he promoted amnesty for any immigrant who'd entered the country before 1 January 1982, which became The Immigration Reform and Control Act (IRCA) on 6 November 1986. The following year, Reagan issued an Executive Order to cover the children of those granted amnesty.

 In 1984, Reagan had made his position clear, by saying: "*I believe in the idea of amnesty for those who have put down roots and lived here, even though sometime back they may have entered illegally.*" But, to gain amnesty, Reagan had promised: "*there would be tighter security at the Mexican border, and employers would face strict penalties for hiring undocumented workers."* Those employer penalties became law, and in 2019 that meant those crossing the border under a claim of asylum were not allowed to be employed until their claim had been vetted and the necessary form of documentation issued.

Having been granted amnesty once, it was clear there was the possibility of a second reprieve and so the number of illegals began to climb. A PEW Research study, dated 3 December 2018, reported that 26.6% of all immigrants – about 12 million – are from Mexico, and of those, 5.4 million are illegal and account for 51% of illegals living in the United States. But, Mexicans citizens no longer constitute the majority of illegals apprehended along the Southern border – the majority are Central and South Americans who passed through Mexico.

Walls do have their place in history. They serve a purpose that we would rather deny. Through denial, we can open the door to an influx of millions. They will come. The denied reality that is associated with Climate Change will assure it. Those honestly seeking Immigration Reform will support Trump and Sanders – they will gut Pelosi, Schumer, and anyone else who disregards the demographic reality accompanying a reality of global populations in transition.

In Biblical times, borders were vague and the walls defined cities. Pence and his Evangelical buddies are required to behave toward immigrants in a very specific manner, it is in Leviticus 19:33, *"When a stranger sojourns with you in your land, you shall not do him wrong. You shall treat the stranger who sojourns with you as the native among you,..."*

In Hebrews 13:2 there is a warning: *"Do not neglect to show hospitality to strangers, for thereby some have entertained angels unawares."*

But no verse prohibits construction of a wall to control the traffic; all the cities had walls and city gates – some called *"eye of the needle,"* because they were designed to restrict traffic to a pace that is easily supervised. But, in the Trump era, Congress opposed honest immigration reform and also vehemently refused proper funding of immigrant processing and assimilation. These are not things a President should request, it is funding the Construction says originates with Congress.

For Reagan, IRCA represented a way to regain control of the borders, with the hope that employers would subsequently be held responsible for employing illegals. As Reagan said, *"It will remove the incentive for illegal immigration by eliminating the job opportunities which draw illegal aliens here."*

On 24 June 2009, Chuck Schumer, one of the sponsors of the 2006 Secure Fence Act, stated in an immigration speech, *"People who enter the United States without our permission are illegal aliens and illegal aliens should not be treated the same as people who enter the United States legally."* Four years later, in June 2013, Schumer was pushing to expand the Wall – but, when Trump accepted all of Schumer's arguments, suddenly Schumer was effectively opposing his own position and inviting them in.

In 2009, Schumer declared: *"When the President asks me whether Congress can pass comprehensive immigration reform this Congress, I will smile and say, 'Mr. President, yes we can. All of the fundamental building blocks are in place to pass comprehensive immigration reform this session and, even possibly, later this year.'"*

In 2018, it was Trump who owned an immigration problem that the Democrats had been trying to address for four decades – over that period, Reagan-Republicans opposed them. But when there was a Republican who took control of the descenders, then agreed with the Democratic position and was willing to wear the mantel of the battle for the WALL, then, suddenly, those seeking reform and control became Reagan-Democrats and rejected the decades of logic and striving for rational policies. Suddenly, it was they who wanted open borders.

Of course, Walls do not keep out Terrorists or Disease, they only direct the carriers to locations where they can be discovered. Michele Obama had said the same thing in a June 2016 speech at City College of New York. But the critical point is the Democratic rejection and refuting of the decades-old Democratic position and accepting the position taken by Ronald Reagan in 1980. Sanders, in taking the nomination leadership, has shown he does not accept destructive optics.

Curiously, the Obama supported 2006 legislation originally called on the Department of Homeland Security to install at least two layers of reinforced fencing along some stretches of the border – basically, the "Wall" Trump promised to build, and the structure eighty Senators, including Clinton, Obama, Schumer, voted for.

Five years later, the media would report that, in a speech given "*in El Paso on immigration reform on May 10, 2011, President Obama declared that the fence along the border with Mexico is 'now basically complete.*'" But, that was only 649 miles of the authorized 652 miles of fence along a 1,954 border, but it was located along the heavily trafficked California border and just north of the heavily concentrated Mexican Drug Cartel operations.

By the standards applied to Trump, Obama lied. However, while the wall or fence did help control traffic into California, it had no real effect on the flow of drugs. It did cut the flow of illegal migration by single males, but a change in Congressional rhetoric resulted in children being sent or brought across the border. The California Court has determined a claim of "asylum" supersedes any and all border control efforts – ultimately, it could negate any concept involving a visa or passport.

In October 2006, when Obama stood on the floor of the Senate and claimed, "*better fences and better security along our borders .... help stem some of the tide of illegal immigration in this country.*" But returning to the 'apprehension' levels existing before the 2006 Secure Fence Act seems to be a common goal of the Pelosi Congress and the California Court, at a time when civil unrest, economic collapse, and Climate Change are combining to motivate Latin Americans to relocate North.

The same thing is happening in Europe, where economic inequality and migration are driving a Nationalist backlash which is being complicated by BREXIT. But, indicators point to the idea that the driving force behind the BREXIT movement is tied to the Russian interference which motivated the Mueller probe. In both instances, the idea is not to achieve a concrete result, but rather to promote economic disruption and political dissension which then destroys the foundation of a targeted nation through a disruption of the core elements of the social fabric.

As events and history will affirm, Schumer and others have taken it upon themselves to do a complete reversal of Democratic objectives of the past four decades. We have also seen attacks on the Constitution. At the same time, where Mueller's investigation should have been focused on the Russian acts of interference that have been documented since the 1960s, the media has converted the process to one of undermining Presidential legitimacy.

We also need to recognize the close parallels between the United States and Britain which make them susceptible to Russian manipulation.

Britain's Chancellor of the Exchequer Philip Hammond, said, "*We are working hard to build a stronger, fairer economy – dealing with the deficit, helping people to work, and cutting taxes for individuals and businesses.*" Do these words differ from anything that has repeatedly been asserted by American political aspirants? All things economic are a threat to Russia, which went bust in 1998.

The Russian economy is not designed to function properly and never was. Historically, Russia depended upon the Pale of Settlement – the Eastern European territory and nations founded by Jewish and Viking merchants, which, the 19th-century Czarina Catherine the Great determined a natural location to both isolate and profit from Jewish capitalists in an anti-Semitic world. Hitler ended the era, but in creating the Soviet Union, an oblivious Stalin became reliant upon Jewish scientists to compete with America's Jewish scientists – for those opposed to anti-Semitism, it became an inside joke.

If it was conducted properly, and with due diligence, the Mueller investigation would establish the timeline that began in 1956, with the boast attributed to Khrushchev: "*We won't have to fight you. We'll so weaken your economy until you'll fall like overripe fruit into our hands.*" And, certainly, it would reference the 1964 quote which is applicable to the attacks on Trump: "*The press is our chief ideological weapon.*"

That weapon is being used to distract from the emergency situation at the Mexican Border. Part of that distraction can be seen in those Members of Congress who consistently harp on the idea of "Children in Cages." They are obfuscating and covering for their failure to do the job for which they were elected – a job that involves proper immigration reform and preparing the nation for the coming problems related to Climate Change.

For those who have yet to grasp the reality, in March 2019 there were 100,000 border apprehensions; the annual peak was attained when 1.61 million were apprehended in 2000 – becoming a justification for the 2006 Secure Fence act. Annualized, March indicated the crisis was on track to add the population of New York City every five years – America's incompetent Legislators are not dealing with absorbing and integrating those numbers into the American population and society.

Instead, the legislature is performing in the manner that Russia and other "bad actors" rely upon to eventually undermine the economy. Congress is in "Climate Denial," and that means they fail to recognize the true nature of the growing emergency at the Southern Border, an emergency that will impact Mexico to an even greater degree.

As of Trump's claim of a border crisis, asylum seekers were arriving from between ten and fifteen degrees north latitude. As the planet warms, equatorial temperatures will reach 120 degrees Fahrenheit (50 degrees Celsius) – the recommended maximum safe temperature for household hot water or equivalent of living in Death Valley National Park.

As the second 57-week cycle ended, Hitler's *Mein Kampf* was invoked by five-term Alabama Republican congressman "Mo" Brooks, who, in reference to Attorney General Barr's summary of the Mueller Report, sought to affirm that the media speculation of collusion between Russia and Trump to influence the election was an example of what Hitler had termed the "Big Lie."

To that end, Brooks Quoted Hitler: "*In the big lie, there is always a certain force of credibility; because the broad masses of a nation are always more easily corrupted in the deeper strata of their emotional nature than consciously or voluntarily; and thus in the primitive simplicity of their minds they more readily fall victims to the big lie than the small lie.*"

Of course, Hitler simply recognized or expressed what had been long known – the bigger the lie, the more easily people come to accept it. Brooks was actually utilizing the technique, to make a false connection between Hitler, Socialism, Progressives, media, and Democrats. He also compared Latin American immigrants to the terrorist attacks on 11 September 2001 and claimed there was a "war on whites" being conducted by the Democratic Party. At the same time, Brooks spoke of the looming financial disaster represented by the debt which Ronald Reagan triggered but now is blamed upon the Democratic propensity to support the biblical common sense associated with lifting people out of poverty and providing them with the healthcare needed to allow them to work.

Like so many others in Congress, Brooks was intentionally invoking emotionality, so as to distract from reality. On 26 March he stood on the floor of the House and presented charts affirming the deficits were growing the National Debt to the point where, in a decade, the related debt service would approach one-trillion dollars. For Brooks, this was a matter of Democrats wanting to provide for the common welfare, rather than pay more for defense than the combined total of the next ten highest military budgets in the world.

Invoking Hitler, the Nazis, or Racism has become a popular means of distracting from reality. Democrats who once promoted the Wall or Fence are now opposing it and pretending there is no border crisis – but do nothing to address the reality represented by the numbers which say nation must prepare to accommodate adding a population equivalent to that of New York City every five years for the next decade or two.

America has the advantage of being surrounded by ocean. That advantage does not exist in Europe, where the refugee and asylum-seeker problem is growing, and actions like BREXIT are serving to complicate matters for Europe. In the meantime, the third cycle began with a shakeup at the Department of Homeland Security – the resignation of its head, Kirstjen Nielsen, who was replaced by acting DHS secretary, Kevin McAleenan.

McAleenan addressed an issue consistently touched on in this book series, only he referenced International studies involving the effect Climate Change related drought and the decline in coffee prices have had on the ability of rural Latin American families to provide for themselves. By addressing this reality, we gain insight into the changes at DHS:

"What we looked at over the last several years is really a

changing demographic coming from Central America, not arriving from the big cities, but primarily, now, we're seeing from Guatemala and Honduras, folks from rural areas.

"These areas are facing significant challenges with food insecurity.

"We're seeing that directly translate into who's arriving at our border. About 30 percent of the arrivals last year were from Guatemala and the vast majority of those arrivals were from the Western Highlands. We're also seeing the rural areas of Honduras coming into play here on the border with Guatemala, where they also were in that Dry Corridor that has faced drought and having challenges with food insecurity. So, really, the hunger concern has become a real prevalent push factor from our analysis and perspective."

Trump, being Trump, distracted media attention with the announcement of a plan to stop roughly one billion dollars in approved financial aid to three Central American countries that are the primary origin of the asylum seekers. Those programs could, temporarily, mitigate the current number of migrants from those nations. But that would only distort the optics or perception of the scope of the growing crisis – allowing the Congressional con artists to put off addressing the issue at a point in time when it can be addressed.

The three nations – El Salvador, Guatemala, and Honduras – collectively designated "the Northern Triangle" have a combined population of 25 million people who, over the next two decades, will be displaced by the effects of Climate Change. For all the rhetoric about Global Warming, Congress has done nothing that will address the related issues. If we look at the Swamp Denizen focus – the idea of impeaching whoever was elected in 2016 – we see a Congress that is intentionally putting matters off, so as to inflict the most harm to the most people.

In a tweet dated 8:27 AM - 23 May 2014, Trump revealed one of his techniques: *"Sometimes by losing a battle, you find a new way to win the war. Don't ever get down on yourself, just keep fighting - in the end, you WIN!"* The issue is, what is the war that he is fighting? Is it the one we think we see him fighting?

CHAPTER TWELVE – Summit Border

"Throughout the centuries there have been men who took the first steps down new roads armed with nothing but their own vision."

~ Ayn Rand

On 11 June 2018 Kim Jong-un and Donald J Trump meet in Singapore; back home in the good old U.S. of A, actor Robert De Niro stepped onto the Tony Award stage and twice shouted out 'Fuck Trump!' Forcefully, De Niro demonstrated that his typical movie role characters were simply variations on the character he is ion his daily life: "I'm going to say this—FUCK TRUMP! It's no longer 'Down with Trump,' it's FUCK TRUMP!"

Of course, the censors bleep it, but De Niro made his point – the fact that Donald Trump was making history certainly rated a "Fuck Trump" or two. And it did get De Niro a standing ovation.

Unless that history marks the beginning of some endless, pointless, undeclared war against a nation that had done nothing to America – Americans hate history being made. Especially if it is connected to formally ending a war that had been on hold for seven decades. So his audience applauded him for insulting their president, and the World had a laugh, before settling back to see what emerged from the Singapore Summit.

When an agreement was signed, MSNBC's Rachel Maddow and producer Steve Benen expressed their usual "it's all bad" slant on all things Trump and characterized the first meeting between a North Korean leader and Superpower Leader of the Free World as ostensibly being "to push the United States' broader goal of denuclearization." And, lacking any specific worthy of attack, they declared "the summit in Singapore fell far short" and should have produced some ironclad roadmap to success.

They quoted then attacked this post-meeting interview:

STEPHANOPOULOS: [North Koreans] have to get rid of all their nuclear weapons?

TRUMP: They have to get rid of, yeah, I think that they will. I really believe that he will. I've gotten to know him well in a short period of time.

STEPHANOPOULOS: Did [Kim] tell you that?

TRUMP: Yeah, he's de-nuking, I mean he's de-nuking the whole place. It's going to start very quickly. I think he's going to start now.

Yet, even though the world was witness to the destruction of Korea's nuclear test site – which clearly happened before, and was a prelude to, the summit agreement – they denied "Korea is "now" in the process of getting rid of its nuclear program."

With this 12 June 2018 enumeration, under a Benen byline, their anti-Trump position promoted the "Fuck Trump" idea:

1. Trump's understanding of current events has reached a delusional stage, and he actually believes his own rhetoric.

2. Kim Jong-un quietly told the American president that his denuclearization efforts are poised to begin, hoping Trump would actually believe this.

3. Trump just made this up.

Throughout the first five books in this series, whenever the topic touched on Korea, it has been clear that there is a two-prong approach to Trump's negotiating style: 1. Be positive, 2. allow the other party to "save face."

Unless it is necessary to demonstrate a clear "push-back" which affirms a meeting of equals, you do not insult or otherwise undermine the other party. And certainly, one should never seek to undermine the authority of their own representative – but, both Maddow and elements of Congress were making it a point to both insult and threaten with impeachment the President, as he was in the process of allowing North and South Korea to come together in a way that would also formalize an end to the Korean War.

On 14 June, after previously reporting Kim had been the one in control – based on Trump announcing he would end "War Games" with South Korean and the summit had yielded no hard and fast denuclearization process, the media quietly reported that the economic sanctions were to remain in place until such time as the DPRK achieves full denuclearization.

The "Fuck Trump" media basically ignored US Secretary of State Mike Pompeo saying: "President Trump has been incredibly clear about the sequencing of denuclearization and relief from the sanctions. ... But we have made very clear that the sanctions and the economic relief that North Korea will receive will only happen after the full..., the complete denuclearization of North Korea."

The Boston Globe proclaimed: "President Trump returned from the Singapore summit with North Korean strongman Kim Jong Un more exposed than ever, with the method of his presidency confirmed — not as a master of the art of the deal but the kind of salesman who gives them all a bad name."

The Globe writer went on to say: "Unlike Trump, of course, Kim's life has been about the use of power in all of its forms. Where Trump was the heir to a Brooklyn-based real estate promoter, Kim was the third in a family line of brutal dictators who was groomed to lead a pariah state in a hostile world."

Of course, American media fails to grasp the reality that being a third generation dictator, with the power to kill all who oppose you, is far easier than being a NYC Real Estate developer.

Ignoring the reality that sanctions were to remain, the Globe writer asserted: "The end of the summit found Russia and China moving to ease sanctions on North Korea and Trump returning to Washington with little more than his claim to a new friendship with Kim Jong Un. The outcome was consistent with his lifelong record to loudly voiced claims of deal-making prowess and the kind of middling results that created a string of embarrassing bankruptcies. The depths to which the salesman was willing to go, in pursuit of nothing more than a photo op, show that it's Kim who knows how to make a deal."

Yes! It was a photo-op. It was a media event Trump had carefully planned and structured to make Kim look good. Prior to the summit, Trump had said he was working without notes and was taken to task for that. But, a year before, on page 66 of book two of the Trump Card series, "Seeking a TRUMP CARD" – as part of the explanation of Trump's North Korean tactic – it states, "If you can sell the idea of irrationality, or spontaneity, as a driving force, behind your decision-making process and use of violence, your opponent tends to either back off or hesitate."

Three pages later, readers were told that "Trump had no interest in the drama associated with putting 'Boots on the ground.'" Clearly, this meant that War Games were pointless in an environment where an angered United States, pushed into defending South Korean, could simply launch missiles from any of numerous points in continental America, and nuke the nuclear-armed DPRK out of existence.

But the Dump Trump types like the idea of boots on the ground, they like sending their neighbor's kids off to die. And, for all of them who call having Bone Spurs draft dodging, what they are really saying is that they approved of murdering Vietnamese who simply wanted Europeans out of their country.

Both Trump and Kim want peace on the peninsula, and by the time of the December 2018 G-20 meeting, things were moving smoothly and Trump asked South Korean President Moon Jae-in to relay a message of friendship to North Korean leader Kim Jong-Un, one which expressed Trump's hope they can "fully carry out the remaining {June Summit} agreements together with him so that he will make Chairman Kim Jong Un get what he wants."

But, readers of the early Trump Card books know this is the mutual goal – all parties, including South Korea, will get achieve the mercantile conclusion which will benefit them all, and then allow China its place in the economic mosaic defining the balance of the 21st-century.

There was always the idea – that any random court action against Trump, his Foundation, or some business interest would provide a basis for impeachment proceedings which would then see Mike Pence installed as POTUS. The Swamp Denizens hidden among the Democrats need a POTUS Pence – a man who is easily attacked using traditional methods and basic simpleton dialogues which allow separating the Evangelicals from the rest of the voter base. If they are lucky, Pence might even reignite the Korean War and crash the economy – he could be another Bush-43.

There was also the idea Trump would buy-into the Right-wing warmonger mentality. It was what South Carolina Senator Lindsey Graham had in mind when he advised the President to be belligerent, after all, "If a million people are going to die, they're going to die over there, not here." He even told Trump that we needed to get rid of Kim Jong-un, that "China needs to kill him and replace him with a North Korean general they can control ...

they need to take him out. Not us, them. And control the nuclear inventory there."

Of course, China had to do it. An Executive Order issued by Gerald Ford on 18 February 1976, banned political assassination and Ronald Reagan affirmed it on 4 December 1981. Then Bush-43 established the United States could use its military to murder a national leader, even though sponsoring a covert effort remained unacceptable.

Politically, give China control of the North Korean military dictatorship and allow China to select a new Supreme Leader who will expand the nuclear program, and POTUS Pence could impose sanctions and, ideally, trigger a nuclear war.

Those who paid attention to the media knew the Denizens of the Swamp deeply desired chaos – economic, military, or social, the important thing is to stop the government from functioning. The Mexican Border crisis will provide millions of individuals who can create localized economic burdens to contribute to the desired levels of chaos.

Of course, The Denizens deny existence of a crisis, and when I was revealed that Trump suggested housing migrants in sanctuary cities, the Denizens went all NIMBY (Not In My Back Yard); the next day there was a report that the Executive Office for Immigration Review issued a deportation order that would send an 11-year-old girl, but not her family, back to El Salvador. This is real child and family separation, and it is on the Congress who have failed to recognize the problem and failed to appropriate the funds to properly staff the agencies responsible for processing the Northern Triangle asylum seekers.

On hearing of notice, an immigration attorney working the border cases noted how chaotic the immigration courts system had become, and described individuals being given incorrect court dates, and clerical errors with consequences including deportation orders where there should not have been any. The attorney also indicated that it was not uncommon for children to be deported alone – as Obama had said he would do when declaring he would put the children back across the border. Other legal experts who are familiar with the actual process, rather than denizen rhetoric, noted child deportation was, in accordance with the Obama policy, typically done with unaccompanied minors.

The way America treats people at the border, and what, on 12 April 2019, USA Today reported as [the] "Democrats denounce White House idea to release migrants in sanctuary cities," shows that those attacking Trump are hypocrites and not to be trusted.

If those who, for decades, called for a border fence/wall are now going to oppose their own border control policy, and then are seen proceeding to complicate matters by rejecting responsibility for processing and accommodating the migrants they have loudly proclaimed are welcome, can any world leader trust them to honor their international policies?

House Speaker Pelosi and her band of denizens choose to attack Trump because they both want the border open to asylum seekers and designated Sanctuary Cities where the undocumented can avoid legal processing – but only so long as no asylum seekers are sent to live in those cities. Note, "sanctuary cities" are places that willfully disregard the law and fail to cooperate with federal immigration enforcement authorities. But they do so in a manner that defies a definitive legal definition and then attack the Trump Administration for seeking one.

On 12 April, a Trump Tweet phrased it this way: "Due to the fact that Democrats are unwilling to change our very dangerous immigration laws, we are indeed, as reported, giving strong considerations to placing Illegal Immigrants in Sanctuary Cities only...."

On 7 April, Bernie Sanders was asked about his position on open borders and denied he supported them, then saying, "I think what we need is comprehensive immigration reform. If you open the borders, there's a lot of poverty in this world, and you're going to have people from all over the world. And I don't think that's something that we can do at this point. Can't do it."

That is, Sanders effectively agreed with Trump and rejected Pelosi, Schumer, and other Left-wing Swamp Denizens. As might be expected, the denizens immediately criticized Sanders and also pointed out that he sounded like Trump on immigration. But, the record shows, Sanders has long been an opponent of open borders and in 2015 called them a Koch Brothers "right-wing proposal" whose goal was "doing away with the concept of a nation state."

The migrant crisis, as previously noted, is only going to get worse – Climate Change will render the Northern Triangle region uninhabitable with the result that its residents either move north or south. As an equatorial nation, Brazil will also be impacted by the increased heat, and that only exacerbates the various climate-related issues. Then there is a persistent South American pattern of economic, political and social instability which will ensure the migratory direction of choice will be north.

In a broad context, solutions to the immigration policy are rooted in foreign policy and the way the United States addresses the Climate Change issue – the degree to which it advances its use of renewable energy and frees itself from fossil fuels. And while it is coming to grips with reality, nations like North Korea need to tread softly as they move toward a mercantile presence on the global stage.

How does America address real issues when it is populated by Swamp Denizens devoted to amassing excessive military might and impeaching its duly elected President, or, failing to impeach oppose even their own policies when that President also advocates them?

If, for the first time in the nation's history, Impeachment were to be accompanied by a Senate conviction, Right-wing voices who would be guiding POTUS Pence. And, obviously, Pence is desired by the Left-wing, as represented by California's African-American Senator, Maxine Waters, who boasted, when members of the Democratic Leadership tell her to tone down impeachment talk, her reply is, "'impeachment, impeachment, impeachment, impeachment, impeachment, impeachment, impeachment.'"

Waters advises: "If you see anybody from that Cabinet in a restaurant, in a department store, at a gasoline station, you get out and you create a crowd and you push back on them and you tell them they're not welcome anymore, anywhere."

That advise, coming from Waters, has a black-comedy tone, given that, prior to the Civil Rights movement, at a time when the 80-year-old Waters was a teenage girl, that would be the response if she had walked into a "White's Only" store.

Clearly, she has shown that bigotry and stupidity are color blind, but are consistent among those who wish harm on others and the nation – those we can identify as The Most Harm To The Most People Swamp Denizens at a time when the common goal is to Drain The Swamp.

But, as proclaimed by the title of book three in this series, The Swamp Fights Back, and it has an ally popular entertainment media which serves as a common platform for socialization based on propaganda and conditioning over-time. The TV show "Dead Like Me" presented an episode entitled "The Shallow End" {S2:E4, 15 August 2004}, has Georgia 'George' Lass {the title character} talking about a 'fair world' and behind we see a slideshow of Idi Amin, Hitler, and Donald Trump, whose images are accompanied by, "The ass holes are treated like kings."

We have the developed Trump image from 2003/4 which places him in the company of antisemitic icon Adolf Hitler, who died in April 1945, and Idi Amin Dada Oumee, the President of Uganda, who died in August 2003. Of course, it would be thirteen years before Donald John Trump would become President, but it is interesting that there is a weird parallel – Hitler wanted to expel the Jews, Amin sought to expel Asians, and, in 2019, Trump was in the position of following Senator Obama's 15 December 2005 position: "We simply cannot allow people to pour into the United States undetected, undocumented, unchecked, and circumventing the line of people who are waiting patiently, diligently, and lawfully to become immigrants in this country."

Nine years later {21 November 2014} President Obama was saying the same thing in the context of "our immigration system is broken, and everybody knows it. ... When I took office, I committed to fixing this broken immigration system. And I began by doing what I could to secure our borders. ... we'll build on our progress at the border with additional resources for our law enforcement personnel so that they can stem the flow of illegal crossings, and speed the return of those who do cross over." And with that speech, Obama made it clear that he too was expelling people.

Consistent with the pattern, President Trump sent asylum seekers back to Mexico to await hearings on their petitions; then, on 12 April 2019, as the monthly numbers climbed to levels which overtaxed the detention and return system, Trump announced his intention to house asylum seekers in Sanctuary Cities, rather than have them become a further burden for ICE or the military, and also relieve Mexico of any additional burden beyond that which had already been accepted for the housing and supporting those lawfully and properly awaiting processing.

Comically, those who had yelled for open borders and blind admission of any who wanted to enter the United States were the first and quickest to reject the sanctuary option. Their attitude retained the NIMBY approach registered in response to proposals to construct Wind Power turbines along the mountain ranges that were viewed by richer rural residents of California and New York.

In this case, the lack of proper judicial facilities along the border created wait and processing times of up two years. But the Sanctuary Cities, characterized by Pelosi and other NIMBY types as Trump's way to exact revenge on Democratic foes, was viewed by The Transactional Records Access Clearinghouse at Syracuse University as beneficial to asylum seekers and the communities.

It was found that Sanctuary Cities like New York and Los Angeles were 20% less likely to have immigrants arrested while in the community. The district attorney for San Francisco, George Gascon, rejected any political motivation, saying:

"With immigrants being less likely to commit crimes than the U.S.-born population, and with sanctuary jurisdictions being safer and more productive than non-sanctuary jurisdictions, the data damns this proposal as a politically motivated stunt that seeks to play politics with peoples' lives."

This was said in the context of a Trump Tweet which effectively blamed the long-running Obama, now Trump, failure to achieve immigration reform on Obama's own party: "Due to the fact that Democrats are unwilling to change our very dangerous immigration laws, we are indeed, as reported, giving strong considerations to placing Illegal Immigrants in Sanctuary Cities only."

At 9:47 PM - 13 Apr 2019, Trump tweeted, Just out: "The USA has the absolute legal right to have apprehended illegal immigrants transferred to Sanctuary Cities. We hereby demand that they be taken care of at the highest level, especially by the State of California, which is well known or its poor management & high taxes!"

Of course, throughout this book series, we have seen the blame must reside with the Swamp Denizens on both sides of the aisle – Pelosi et al had decided to weaponize those seeking asylum and use them as pawns in their ongoing attacks on Trump.

However, rational minds have pointed out that these cities have robust networks of nonprofit legal groups with the skills and knowledge to help asylum seekers build strong legal cases which would result in asylum being granted. In a related tweet, Trump wrote, "The Radical Left always seems to have an Open Borders, Open Arms policy - so this should make them very happy!". But the fact is, those Trump calls "The Radical Left" and I call Swamp Denizens, are not interested in these individuals receiving the best possible [an free] legal assistance, rather they want them detained in poorly funded "concentration camp" environments – which the media can then report about in terms of "children in cages".

During a 2012 campaign stop in Maine, Obama entered the group when, during a speech on the economy, he mentioned the 2009 film "Up In The Air" – one of the stars, Anna Kendrick, was in the audience. Afterward, they talked and she related the story on "The Late Show With Stephen Colbert" recalling: "So, I called him an 'asshole,' and scolded him for not knowing the 50 states. LUCKILY...he has a great sense of humor and clearly took it well."

The fifty state reference was to a comment made during a 9 May 2008 campaign stop in Oregon, when Obama said, "It is wonderful to be back in Oregon. Over the last 15 months, we've traveled to every corner of the United States. I've now been in 57 states? I think one left to go. Alaska and Hawaii, I was not allowed to go to even though I really wanted to visit, but my staff would not justify it."

From the contextual mention of Alaska and Hawaii, we know this was not, as some have said, a reference to the 57 Islamic States – those with a Muslim majority. Had Trump made such an obvious gaffe, he'd never have heard the end of it.

Setting aside the negative, the "Dead Like Me" writers had clearly grouped Trump with national leaders a dozen years prior to his becoming one. On the other hand, the writers for the adult cartoon series Rick and Morty went to Trump for inspiration and in the episode aired 1 October 2017, "The Rickchurian Mortydate"

S3:E10, in which Obama is depicted using satellite-based invasive infrared video surveillance to illegally spy on grandpa Rick. Later on, Morty accuses Obama of sitting on his ass at peace conferences and tells him, "You Suck!" Later, a naked Obama, by virtue of being POTUS, introduces himself as the "President of the World."

Yet, as "President of the World", Obama was unable to even begin brokering an end to the Korean War or normalize relations on the Korean Peninsula. But, based on William Barr's statement to the Senate subcommittee on 10 April 2019 – "I think spying did occur." – it seems Rick and Morty were on to something.

On 9 September 2018, Trump tweeted an assertion by the former Right-wing Congressman cum Fox News employee Jason Chaffetz:

> "Barack Obama talked a lot about hope, but Donald Trump delivered the American Dream. All the economic indicators, what's happening overseas, Donald Trump has proven to be far more successful than Barack Obama. President Trump is delivering the American Dream."

Of course, Trump hasn't delivered the American Dream – the immigration reform Obama sought but failed to achieve was still elusive. Forcing Congress to deal with asylum migrants might change things but to do that, those who, by law, must be released within 20-days will need to be relocated to Sanctuary Cities. As with Obama, Trump encouraged population demographics to do their thing, while the Swamp Denizens known as the ultra-Right and ultra-Left continue to try to screw things up.

While engaged in the gargantuan effort associated with the process of turning the stampeding, Trump also managed to be a catalyst for peace in Korea. That did not stop him from showing that he didn't mid decisive victories in war – as shown by the use of a MOAB to inflict serious harm on Afghanistan Taliban forces.

As of September 2018, the sum of the Summits amounted to the first inter-Korean summit of late April 2018, which, even as the ultra-Left in America was saying Trump was going to cause a nuclear war, reduced war fears on the peninsula. Then there was a second one in May, which ensured the historic June meeting between Kim Jong-Un and Donald Trump would go off without a hitch. And so set the stage for Trump to say, "We're going to have a great discussion and, I think, tremendous success. It will be tremendously successful. And it's my honor."

In accordance with the rules of the game, explained in the earlier books in this series, it was a great success, with the North Korean people bestowing the title 'Supreme Leader" on Trump – even while the ultra-Left in America attacked Trump as an idiot.

In April 2019, we witnessed the pre-summit posturing that took the form of Kim Jung-un saying: "The US said recently that it is thinking again of a third DPRK-US summit and have been strongly implying problem-solving through dialogue. But they continue to ignore the basic way of the new DPRK-US relations, including withdrawing hostile policies, and mistakenly believe that if they pressure us to the maximum, they can subdue us."

As in America, where the media likes to comment on it, DPRK saw another in a series of high-profile departures among the old guard leadership. This followed upon a new premier being chosen by the government's parliament and leader Kim Jong Un being elected chairman of the State Affairs Commission – a role that was justified by "his outstanding ideological and theoretical wisdom and experienced and seasoned leadership."

While America attempts to get its act together, Kim Jong-un and South Korean President Moon Jae-in were addressing the challenge of creating the written agreement which would formally end the Korean War and achieve denuclearization. Reality has a way of inflicting itself on the fantasy imposed by America media pundits.

North Korea has become, and shall continue to remain, a nuclear power, because there is no rational reason for them to surrender that defensive status – especially in a world that ignores the reality of Pakistan as a nuclear power among Muslims with a bias for terrorism and, in the case of Pakistan, war against Indian Hindus.

CHAPTER THIRTEEN – TRUTH

"No, it isn't truth. Truth isn't truth."
~ **Rudolph William Louis "Rudy" Giuliani**
to NBC's Chuck Todd, 19 August 2018

Is there Truth, when there is Truth to be known and it conflicts with selling newspapers of gaining audience share?

If a habitual liar tells you, "I always lie," aren't they, in fact, telling you the truth? Therefore, simply based on the content of the statement, they are lying by telling you the truth.

As I mentioned on page 180 of *NO TRUMP CARD* – which was published in April 2017 – political lies, like "Lawyer's Lies", are predicated on telling the truth. So it was that I said: it was " demonstrated with a line from the Johnny Depp movie, *Pirates of the Caribbean: 'You lied to me, by telling me the truth.'*"

Trump can say *"the media is the enemy of the people"* and be both a liar and truth teller. When the media engages in tabloid techniques, it lies by telling the truth. When it promotes baseless speculation it is actually engaging in propaganda that, often, has the goal of harming the subject of the conjecture.

Consider the classic example of the journalism question to a politician *"Sir! Are you still beating your wife?"*

Clearly, it's a Catch-22 query. It's a question without any apparent evidentiary basis, and the headline becomes damning, regardless of how the politician chooses to respond. If they don't respond, *"Politician ducks question about ongoing wife beating."* If they deny they ever beat their wife, it's presented as, *"Politician denies still beating his wife."*

The headline is there, the opening condemnation based on a falsely inferred allegation grabs the readers and is implanted in their minds. The article need not follow-up on the matter, rather it will change topic and deal with the other topics discussed – but do so in a manner that infers a ducking of the issue. In the future, the media can keep the issue alive and generate headlines such as, *"Politician continues to evade wife beating issue."*

The Bret Kavanaugh SCOTUS hearings presented a rather

beautiful example of Truth & Lie, in the September 2018 when Dr. Christine Blasey Ford accused Kavanaugh of attempting to rape her when she was 15 and he 17 – both were at a teenage party and, Ford allegedly indicated that Kavanaugh was too drunk to achieve his goal. That goal was sex when she and Kavanaugh apparently were in a bedroom. She claimed he was too drunk to achieve his goal, but didn't relate how drunk she was – or why she had gone into the bedroom with him. Neither were we told many drunken parties either of them routinely attended. A Tabloid might phrase it as "*how many drunken orgies?*"

What we saw was a standard of analysis that explains why juvenile records are sealed. In this case, no formal charges were filed, and it was thirty years ago, so there isn't a claim of even reliable evidence to support a 'she said, he said' debate. What we do know is that the Trump era has created the basis for a rather new standard of judgment – everyone should be judged based on allegations of their behavior as children. Juvenile records, which clearly are firm documentation of behavior, should not be sealed and should be used whenever the character of a job applicant has been deemed a factor in the hiring process.

But, the Kavanaugh confirmation hearings invoked teenage behavior in which the girl was a willing participant, who might not have objected to the 'second base' behavior of a boy, had it not been for another boy being an alleged spectator or participant. As Majority Leader Mitch McConnell proclaimed on the Senate Floor and then Tweeted at 11:20 AM - 25 Sep 2018: "*This is America. Evidence matters. Facts matter. We have never been - and do not wish to be - a society in which a single, uncorroborated allegation can wield veto power over somebody's life. Everyone deserves better than this.*"

We have moved into the next phase of social evolution – it is now becoming apparent, the in-crowd popular party kids are to be excluded from the seats of power. The Kavanaugh test shall be the future. Any teen who belonged to the "popular kids", and then exercised or experimented with their drunken power, will be part of out-crowd. Set aside degrees and adult history, the basis of all evaluations will be based on teen years and teen stupidity. If you are a girl, you get a mandatory pass; if a boy, you're career must be brought to an end. The victor is the boring geek who nobody would associate with in High School, and did nothing that anyone ever noticed – THE GEEKS WIN!

The Kavanaugh case exposed another aspect of reality – we cannot escape our heritage. That's a scary idea and one which will turn many people off, and enrage many others, yet, it seems to be the basis of the Kavanaugh matter, a reason why his High School behavior became relevant.

Having ceded responsibility for vetting Kavanaugh, to his advisers and the Congressional Republican leadership, Trump could wash his hands of personal responsibility. Keeping his neutrality, Trump would say of Ford, "*I thought her testimony was very compelling and she looks like a very fine woman to me. A very fine woman. And I thought that Brett's testimony likewise was, really something that I hadn't seen before. Incredible. It was an incredible moment in the history of our country.*"

Asked if he had something to say to the Senators, he said it fell on them, "*They have to do what they think is right. There is no message whatsoever. They have to do what they think is right. They have to be comfortable with themselves and I'm sure that's what they want.*"

During his testimony, Kavanaugh's Irish temper became obvious and, in response to Senator Dianne Feinstein, he easily admitted, "*Yes, we drank beer. My friends and I, the boys and girls. Yes, we drank beer. I liked beer. Still like beer.*" And with that admission, underscored the fact he was clearly a 19th century drunken Irishman who had risen above his station in life but could not escape his turn of the century stereotypical Irish roots.

Former President George W Bush -- the man who let Bin Laden walk, used the U.S. Military to murder America's Allie against Iran, and contributed to creating The Great Recession -- was actively lobbying for Kavanaugh, who worked as Bush's legal counsel in the 2000 election and Florida "hanging chat" recount which made Bush POTUS -- after which Brett was rewarded with an appointment to the U.S. Circuit Court of Appeals. The Bush endorsement declared him "*a fine husband, father, and friend — and a man of the highest integrity. He will make a superb Justice of the Supreme Court of the United States.*"

This was contrasted by Trump's underscoring differences

between parties with a Tweet saying: *"Judge Kavanaugh showed America exactly why I nominated him. His testimony was powerful, honest, and riveting. Democrats' search and destroy strategy is disgraceful and this process has been a total sham and effort to delay, obstruct, and resist. The Senate must vote!"*

An Irish brawl is riveting; even the term "riveting" provided a subliminal reference to, and invokes, the work done by early Industrial age drunken Irish workers. And with that invocation, Trump approved the called for further FBI investigation which would delay the confirmation vote for a week.

This was not a setback for Trump, his prepared alternate nominee list was said to be composed of conservatives deemed to be credible and class appropriate. candidates worthy of receiving a bipartisan stamp of approval to seal his judicial legacy.

Senator Feinstein commented on Kavanaugh's Irish temper display when she said: *"This was not someone who reflected an impartial temperament or the fairness and evenhandedness one would see in a judge. This was someone who was aggressive and belligerent."*

Senator Lindsey Graham looked at the way the Democrats approached the matter, with the words: *"If you really wanted to know the truth, you sure as hell wouldn't have done what you did to this guy. Boy, you guys want power. God, I hope you never get it. I hope the American people can see through this sham. That you knew about it and you held it. ...To my Republican colleagues, if you vote no, you're legitimizing the most despicable thing I have seen in my time in politics."*

Of course, the voter base for the Republican Party is made up of the modern version of the drunken Irish blue-collar workers; while their bosses are modern anti-union modern slave-masters. But, as the world witnessed, the Democrats are "Boston Brahmin or New England elite" transposed to Maryland and Washington.

The Kavanaugh-Ford controversy is a product of when they were born – they were children of the 'Flower Children'; Brett was born in February 1965, Christine in November 1966, and the event in question allegedly occurred in the summer of 1982. The years are important because they reflect what was acceptable behavior. Culturally acceptable, star creating 'elevator pitch' of the type which might read: *"The sixteen-year-old has a crush on the most popular boy in school, and the geekiest boy in school has a crush on her. ...and we have the makings of a hilarious journey into young womanhood."* In this case, it applies to a teenage romantic comedy released on 4 May 1984, starring Molly Ringwald in the role presented as Dr. Ford's testimony, and Anthony Michael Hall in the role she assigned to Brett Kavanaugh – that of a boy who must secure her panties in order to gain the approval of his peers. The movie is, of course, '*Sixteen Candles*'.

On Saturday, 6 October, the Kavanaugh Confirmation was put to a Senate vote and approved by a 50-48 vote party-line vote – the missing two votes were Montana's Senator Steve Daines, who was at his daughter's wedding "giving away the bride", and Alaska Senator Lisa Murkowski voted "Present," and, therefore, could honestly say she did not vote 'NO'.

After Kavanaugh's Confirmation, President Trump stated to him and the nation:

"I would like to apologize to Brett and his family for the terrible pain and suffering that you have been forced to endure. What happened to the Kavanaugh family violates every notion of fairness, decency and due process.

"In our country, a man or a woman must always be presumed innocent unless and until proven guilty. And with that, I must state that you, sir, under historic scrutiny, were proven innocent."

Of course, the media jumped on the fact that Trump said: *"proven innocent"*. With the world as a witness, it is clear Trump also lied in stating, *"presumed innocent unless and until proven guilty."* Since the era of the Salem Witch Trials, America has been a land where a mere accusation is sufficient to confer guilt. Were America a land of law and justice, a failure to establish clear proof of guilt would – as Trump envisioned and expressed it – amount to proof of innocence.

It is said, *"give me the child for the first eight years of its life, and I will return you the adult."*

Those children born in the 1970s, then raised as part of the privileged echelons, are the ones defining modern global society. But it is a later generation, the one seen in the streets, that is defining the Rule of Law – or, more accurately, the lack of any Rule of Law for those who, in 2050, will be the ones defining both America and global society as a Universal Fascist Culture in which any person guilty because one person said so, and the Emperor's mob accepts what it is told.

Think about the mentality of the period from 1964 to 1974, where July 1972 marked counterculture actress Jane Fonda visiting North Vietnam and thereafter being "Hanoi Jane" within the pro-war Republican Vietnam lexicon. Nixon signed the Paris Peace Accords on 27 January 1973; this was the first government action toward ending direct U.S. involvement in Vietnam; in 1974, Nixon resigned; then, eight months later, Saigon fell and America witness the embarrassing 18-hour mass evacuation from the roof of its Embassy – events which weighed heavily on those families involved in Washington politics.

In 1990, Bill Clinton summarized the period with the words: "*If you look back on the Sixties and think there was more good than bad, you're probably a Democrat. If you think there was more harm than good, you're probably a Republican.*"

The controversy is derived from Democrats realizing the bad elements of the period – the rebellion and 'free love' parties related to illegal drugs – augmented by booze – which, by 1982, saw private school elite teens using alcohol as the basis for demonstrating a rebellion their preschooler selves were carefully taught was proper. Today, we look at their children playing a #METOO game, attacking the elite of their parents' generation in the same was elite has always been created and then attacked.

Trump tweeted this idea when he wrote: "*You don't hand matches to an arsonist and you don't give power to an angry left-wing mob - and that's what they've become. The Democrats have become too extreme and too dangerous to govern. Republicans believe in the rule of law, not the rule of the mob.*"

Are Democrats *"too dangerous to govern"*? Moreover, are we even talking about the actions of Democrats? Have Democrats even shown the coherence necessary to apply such a broad brush to those who began attacking Trump on 6 November 2016, and who are already calling for Kavanaugh's impeachment admit rants about protecting "rapists", when there was no rape?

In the Trump era, the world is witness to the next stage of the sixties era mentality being adopted as the basis for reporting on Trump Administration practices. Republican Trump can do no right, Black Democrat Obama can do no wrong.

When a woman makes an assertion, without evidence, she is to be believed and the male, regardless of known facts, cannot be believed. That both were engaged in gender-specific versions of the exact same behavior, the woman is exempt, because, as the 1960s taught us, a white male Republican elite that controls all things and loves to get America into wars.

Today, a Left-wing elite can yell about human rights, while denying basic human rights, because women must be believed, even as they admit to being 15-years old and attending drunken-teen parties the specifics of which they do not recall, and nobody else can confirm. In 1985, drinking to excess was the norm, but by 2005 only 43% of 16 to 26-year-olds did so; by 2015, that number was down to 28% and, as marijuana is legalized in more states, the numbers will continue to fall while many embark on a lifetime as healthy Trump-style teetotalers.

On 6 October, the day before the Senate Confirmation vote, Journalist Stephanie Gutmann told the Guardian, a 200-year old British newspaper, *"We have husbands and sons and brothers and lovers and they're part of our lives intertwined. I think it's fair to have the emphasis on sons now because the ball swings back and forth and right now the pendulum has swung way too far in the sort of believe-the-woman-at-any-cost direction."*

From a legal viewpoint, Senate GOP outside counsel Rachel Mitchell summed things up in a formal memo which stated: *"Dr. Ford identified other witnesses to the event, and those witnesses either refuted her allegations or failed to corroborate them. ... I do not think that a reasonable prosecutor would bring this case based on the evidence before the Committee. Nor do I believe that this evidence is sufficient to satisfy the preponderance-of-the-evidence standard."*

On 9 October, Hillary Clinton pipped in with the assertion that Trump had turned Kavanaugh's ceremonial swearing-in into a staged *"political rally"* which *"further undermined the image and integrity of the court."* In truth, Clinton was arguing the idea that, 35-years after the fact, teenagers are to be deemed guilty until proven innocent and that exposing this reality undermines a false *"image and integrity"* claimed for a judicial system known for its race-based bigotry.

Clinton, who ignored her husband's proven infidelities, was playing to the demonstrators, she asserted the failure to destroy a man's reputation based on unsubstantiated claims of behavior over three decades earlier *"troubles me greatly. It saddens me. Because our judicial system has been viewed as one of the main pillars of our constitutional government. So I don't know how people are going to react to it. I think, given our divides, it will pretty much fall predictably between those who are for and those who are against."*

While Clinton was focused on teenage behavior thirty-five years in the past, the media was reporting on Climate change and the ineffectiveness of the Paris Accord targets which were going to shape the Global environment twenty to thirty years in the future. Nobody was demonstrating to save the planet, it was obviously far more important to rant about the unsubstantiated claims of a 50-year-old talking about events when they were fifteen. American values and priorities were being made clear to the world – future life on the planet is trivial and meaningless when compared to the opportunity to wage a politically based attack.

Were we watching something other than Democrats trying to play the devil's witch hunt games, there would be evidence and not the admission that, as a teenage girl, Ford knowingly attended a regular weekly summer drinking party involving four in-crowd high school seniors and one other girl – the purpose of which was to get drunk while making-out. Fortunately, twenty-first-century rationality dismisses reality, applies modern standards to the past, and disregards the realities of the present – accordingly, we see the Ford story and vandalism associated with historic monuments attacks.

We saw this with the strict immigration policies touted by both Barack Obama and Chuck Schumer. When Trump adheres to them, when he wants credit for completing and improving the structure that was authorized under the 2006 SECURE FENCE ACT, and calling it a Wall rather than Fence, he was attacked.

Among the attackers was Senate Minority Leader Charles E. "Chuck" Schumer, who, apparently out of political spite, was attacking his own legislative agenda, because he would rather not have it achieved than see his work become Trump's Legacy. It is also worth noting that Schumer was first elected to Congress when Ronald Reagan entered the White House. Reagan opposed the Border Fence and proposed amnesty for those "undocumented" immigrants who, in a passionate speech, Schumer insisted be called what they were – illegally here in violation of American law. In 2018, Schumer sounded like Reagan, because Trump was the one presenting Schumer's platform from pre-1980 and well into the Obama era.

How honest is Schumer? His voting record shows, in 1996 he was for The Defense of Marriage Act (DOMA) which, in 2013, was later found unconstitutional, in part based on the constraints imposed on the benefits received by, and the rights afforded, legally married same-sex couples. So he was an anti-homosexual Democrat who sided with far-right evangelical bigots.

By March 2009, the political tides had changed and we see Schumer had reversed himself and was supporting then same-sex marriages he had previously opposed. One might infer a pattern: in 1996, Clinton was in office; in 2009, Obama had not yet been elected and Bush was in the White House, so Schumer was making himself compatible with the next POTUS. In which case, his pre-2016 positions were based on the assumption of a Clinton victory.

In 2013, Schumer was part of the bipartisan Gang of Eight promoting a Senate initiated Immigration Reform bill designed to grant undocumented immigrants with legal status and eventually citizenship – an idea initiated by Ronald Reagan, but introduced under President Obama. The bill passed the Senate with a strong 68-32 majority but died in the House of Representatives, when Speaker John Boehner refused to take up the legislation.

It's interesting that the Bill was entitled "Border Security, Economic Opportunity, and Immigration Modernization Act of 2013" and basically would have established the very policies that Donald Trump has promoting. Effectively, Schumer is opposing his own 2013 legislative initiative.

The record shows Trump has argued for putting an end to

the *Diversity Visa Lottery* and instituting a program designed to provide green cards to immigrants with advanced skills. This was integral to the 2013 legislation, as were provisions Trump has sought for Stronger border security and law enforcement. DACA, had come into existence on 15 June 2012, Schumer's legislation would have made it legal, and the bi-partisan committee convened by Trump would have been empowered to make it legal – but the world saw Schumer tie the matter to the Budget, rather than pass a simple agreed to legislative package based on his own 2006 and 2013 positions.

Since funding the "Wall" – the steel concrete and slat Fence – was simply full funding for existing law, there was no basis for a budgetary problem. Especially since that legislation was the product of work by Senators Schumer, Clinton and Obama, and had the full support of the Republicans.

In 1980, when an audience member asked, *"Do you think the children of illegal aliens should be allowed to attend Texas public schools free or do you think that their parents should pay for their education?"*

Candidate George Herbert Walker Bush responded:

"If they're living here, I don't want to see 6- and 8-year-old kids being made totally uneducated and made to feel like they're living totally outside the law. These are good people, strong people."

Candidate Ronald Wilson Reagan responded:

"Rather than talking about putting up a fence, why don't we work out some recognition of our mutual problems? Make it possible for them to come here legally with a work permit. And then, while they're working and earning here, they can pay taxes here. And then when they want to go back, they can go back. Open the borders both ways."

What is "Truth"? As Giuliani said, "Truth isn't Truth." Truth is what sells today, and yesterday was a lie to be ignored.

In Act 5 scene 1 of "Measure for Measure", Shakespeare had Isabella say:

> *"Than this is all as true as it is strange:*
> *Nay, it is ten times true; for truth is truth*

To the end of reckoning."

To this Duke Vincentio declares:

Away with her! Poor soul,

She speaks this in the infirmity of sense.

Of course, a few statements later, Isabella says:

O gracious duke,

Harp not on that, nor do not banish reason

For inequality; but let your reason serve

To make the truth appear where it seems hid,

And hide the false seems true

The debate over truth hinges on reason, and reason can be lost when people give in to bias or inequity – that bias emerges as the failure to treat all parties, all sides, equally.

People have pointed to First Lady Melania Trump recycling or plagiarizing Michelle Obama. But that ignores a time-honored reality based on the idea that, if something works, don't change it.

Melania's actions were no different than those which define the surface image of the Trump Campaign and the way he won the POTUS race – as seen in the "*Make America Great Again*" slogan.

Before we look at #MAGA, let's take a quick look at Reagan and something he said in a campaign ad Statue of Liberty voice-over in which he is pro-immigration and effectively grabbed the classic line from the inauguration speech of John F Kennedy: "*ask not what your country can do for you, ask what you can do for your country.*"

When Reagan used it with #MAGA, it came across like this:

"Through this Golden Door has come millions of men and women. These families came here to work. Others came to America and often harrowing conditions. They didn't ask what this country could do for them but what they could do to make this refuge the greatest home of freedom in history. They brought with them courage and the values of family, work, and freedom. Let us pledge to each other that we can make America great again."

The #MAGA slogan is recycled (in terms of what has been said of Melanie speeches, plagiarized) from the past successful campaign by Reagan. It's Republican/Conservative because it's from the Republican Conservative icon and entertainment type.

What it means is a subliminal variation on what Reagan used it to mean. In 1980, Reagan was entering at the end of the frustrating Cold War era. Iran has taken hostages and Carter was not a warmonger, so they had no fear of him.

Before Carter, the Vietnam "War" has seen Americans running with tails between legs (something historians and political analysts knew would happen —because they had held the French a bag for a generation — but which was suppressed from public knowledge).

The GREATNESS that America had felt as being the determining force in the 1st and 2nd world war had melted away. Reagan latched on to that feeling and so proclaimed LET'S MAKE AMERICA GREAT. A very positive and clear objective, in terms of how the Baby-Boomers should feel about themselves and the nation.

All the racist negatives thrown at Obama (by those same Republicans) degraded the national feeling. Plus, Baby- Boomers were now facing retirement — in 2015, they started turning 70 — and were looking back at what they achieved or failed to achieve. A very depressing reality, even for those who achieved a lot. Their parents were dead, childhood friends were dead, spouses had died, things were changing rapidly, and retirement meant a new unknown reality for which few had role models. We forget, by the time they were 35–25, half of the global population, those born in their birth year, were dead.

Trump grabbed a slogan that worked, and said, let's do it again — which also meant win as Reagan had. And it worked. Trump's a salesman, he knows slogans and knows to do what worked in the past. He does that repeatedly. LOL which is what he gets attacked for, and why the attacks are generally doomed to failure... they too are the same old attacks.

Around 11 May 2018, a QUORA discussion groups question raised the issue of Trump's "lies". That night, while laying in bed and trying to sleep, it dawned on me that lies ensure reelection.

I realized Nixon, George W Bush, Bill Clinton, and, with BIRTHER movement saying he lied about where he was born, and people calling him a liar with Obama care related statements like, '*If you like your health care plan, you can keep it*', and there were internet sites which, during his first term in the POTUS office, had published lists of alleged lies he told.

Each of the POTUS who were, in recent history elected to a second term, share the common a common reality – they were all branded liars. That common reality infers that only liars are rewarded with a second term in the Oval Office.

Jimmy Carter was hyper-honest so only survived one term; during his first term, George HW Bush wasn't called a liar, which resulted in his defeat by Bill Clinton – who, in his second term, was impeached for his lie about Monica and Oral in the Oval. If you don't lie in the first term, it appears people must feel you will in the second.

Based on voter history, the worst thing the Democrats can do is call Trump a liar — it would seem to be sufficient to assure him a 2020 victory... just as feel-good messages win elections.

The #MAGA slogan used first used by Ronald Reagan in the form of "Let's Make America Great Again", was adopted by Donald Trump 35-years later, with the "let's" call for unity and support as an implied mandate.

At its root, the #MAGA slogan is a feel-good mobilization objective which can resonate with individuals in whatever way they wish to interpret it.

When people mobilize around the goal of impeachment, they are screaming a negative, feel bad about the state of the nation, message. Impeach is a message of hate and Constitutional Crisis, which, in the case of Trump, would elevate a theocratic Right-wing individual to presidential power. By having such a person as vice-president, Trump installed an insurance policy of the worst kind – those who successfully attacked him would be responsible for undermining their own security and the future of their children.

Every era that offers up negative vibes will present some form of positive. The Cold War and Korean War era had Milton Berle, Abbott and Costello, Martin and Lewis, or "I Love Lucy" and a range of feel-good TV comedies. In the Trump era, we had a similar reality, one of which highlighted children and presented a vision of the future – Steve Harvey's "Little Big Shots", which presented exceptionally talented and mature children engaged in performances normally associated with adults.

Times have clearly changed; America was at a significant point in its history; the November 2018 election, and Trump Era, were the defining point in America's history – but, to what extent did Trump realize this?

On Friday 21 September, Donald Trump was at a Missouri campaign rally in which he clearly defined the Midterm election: *"Get out in 2018, because you're voting for me in 2018. You're voting for me. You're voting for me."*

Note, not for Republicans, but for Trump. But, as he said, *"To me, it's the Democrat Party, and they aren't just extreme. They are, frankly, dangerous, and they are crazy. They're crazy."*

He was careful to point out we were not talking about the grammatically correct "Democratic Party", but rather, a *Democrat Party* that really showed no interest in the wellbeing of the nation – its only focus was creating a scenario that would bring down the economy, because '*They're crazy.*" While they might be "crazy", was Trump as crazy as they would have people believe?

Supposedly, 43% of Americans supported impeachment with a conviction that would remove him from office. Certainly, he did not want people elected who would support impeachment; at the same time, Trump would not want people who opposed his core goals – which included universal healthcare.

And then we have the reality of the SCOTUS in the current era of the 45th or 46th POTUS. It is a reality defined by the fact that the American life expectancy is 76-78, and two Kavanaugh era justices are an 85-year-old Ruth Bader Ginsburg and an 80-year-old Stephen Breyer. Since both were Democratic appointees, they can be seen as "Liberal."

Clearly, American voters expect one or both to be replaced by Trump appointees who are willing to face anti-Kavanaugh style attacks. It is unlikely the process will be smooth, and highly likely it will push the Court further to the Right.

Were the drive to impeach Trump and replace him with an ultra-Right-wing Mike Pence to succeed, it is clear the Left-wing desires an ultra-Right-wing Supreme Court whose justices would be selected by a theocratic hypocrite. Such a theocratically biased court would interpret or define laws well into the 2050s, and, in effect, subjugate the United States to a modern form of Sharia Law of a type which defined the Inquisitions.

Not that it would really matter. The Impeachment process would end the Obama-Trump economy and plunge both America and Europe into a severe Recession or major Depression. Strict government control would then follow, and the SCOTUS actions would only be noticed by historians writing about the events and causes which led to the Third World War – the Apocalypse that is predicted to occur around 2035.

Throughout the period of the Mueller investigation, many in the media, along with those engaged in conflict politics, ranted about the Mueller Report and how it would show Trump colluded with Russia. But, with its release, and the Barr summary, Truth became reality – voters didn't care about seeing the Report. But, it became clear they did want to see Trump's Tax Returns – they wanted to know how much he made, and gain some basis for the usual gossip about insider elitist wealth.

In the second week of the 3rd 57-week cycle, media reports mentioned the release of the Tax Returns for Senators Warren and Sanders – then focused on Trump repeating that his returns were under audit and so he was not going to release them at the current time. However, the redacted version of the Mueller Report was on the way and so there was ample material for speculation. As far as the returns, it seems, after his failed shot at the Democratic nomination, Bernie Sanders wrote a Best Seller which netted him almost a million dollars in loyalties and quadrupled his net worth.

It would seem there was an interesting beginning to the 3rd 57-week cycle – one made more interesting when, on Income Tax Day {15 April}, during the last week of Catholic Lent, called Holy Week and embodying Palm Sunday, Holy or Spy Wednesday, Holy or Maundy Thursday, Good Friday, and Holy Saturday. It was, on Monday, often designated "Great Monday", that the Cathedral of Notre Dame caught fire.

Relative to 56/57-week cycles, it is interesting that the fire occurred on the last day of the sixth or first day of the seventh 56-week cycle after the 2016 election. An interesting coincidence.

CHAPTER FOURTEEN – 2020 Election
"Wealth is the product of a man's ability to think."
~ Ayn Rand

With Tax Day and the destruction of the Cathedral of Notre Dame we again are faced with the silliness of the 56 and 57-period cycle. It's Stonehenge; it's the Chinese and Hebrew Calendar; it's also the number of Presidential election cycles since the founding of the United States.

But, when it comes to Notre Dame, we have the curiosity of dates. Wikipedia cites a 1980 history book and informs us: "*The chronicler Jean de Saint-Victor [fr] recorded in the Memoriale Historiarum that the construction of Notre-Dame began between 24 March and 25 April 1163 with the laying of the cornerstone in the presence of King Louis VII and Pope Alexander III.*" The laying of the cornerstone is concurrent with the life of Hugh of Cyfeiliog, whose daughters serve as the kinship references in this discussion of POTUS Cousins.

As many know, the French Calendar was reformed in 1563, when King Charles IX changed the start of the year from Easter Day to the January First. Then, on 22 December 1564, the French Parliament turned the edict into law. It took the British roughly 188 years instituted a similar change. Tradition has it that, "April Fools Day" came about when some Frenchmen failed to realize the start of the year had changed.

Regardless of the origin of the foolishness, our interest lays in the fact that both Notre Dame's cornerstone was laid and the fire occurred in the month of April. Today, in 2019, based on the modern calendar system, we might say 856 years had passed, but it might be 855 years. And, if the lower number applies than the fire occurred 15 times 57 years after the laying of the cornerstone.

Concurrent with the fire, there was a fire at the Al-Aqsa Mosque – the third holiest site in Islam, the 'the Farthest Mosque' is located on Jerusalem's Old City Temple Mount. Curiously, if we go back 20 OMER {20 times 49} we find had Al-Aqsa matched to reconstruction of a Jewish Temple, and birth of Shlomo Yitzchaki, known as the Rashi, who, in his French birthplace was known as

Salomon de Troyes – who died roughly sixteen 57-year cycles ago.

Both Liberals and Conservatives are unified by the fact they do not recognize the patterns related to human events. Nor, if we think about it, should they. As we know, the number fifty-seven is another way to say three nineteen Hebrew and Chinese calendar cycles, or one complete cycle embodied in the standing stones at Stonehenge. The OMER is simply an ancient unit of measure that has cultural significance – even among those who are unaware of it.

OMER introduces things that believers in the mystical are obligated to consider – at least in the context of America's 1776 Revolutionary year date.

Five OMER marks 2021, and that marks the next POTUS Administration – a year in which the successful impeachment of Trump would elevate whoever is serving as his Vice President to the Oval Office. It is also a year when a septuagenarian president will occupy the Oval Office, in a nation where the average person of that generation will die between the ages of 76 and 78.

Will Mike Pence succeed Donald Trump? Be it due to a historic House impeachment and Senate conviction, or simply an age and medical condition related event, Pence would represent a historic event – the first President who is not a family member ...mot a POTUS Cousin. Of course, Trump might pull a Nixon and change Vice Presidents – replacing the non-Cousin with a Cousin – and thus ensure that a POTUS cousin continues in the office.

The fate of the Nation could rest on who Trump selects as his running mate. But it also resides in the choices the Democrats make. Will they nominate a POTUS Cousin or repeat what they did with Hillary? The whole POTUS Cousin thing is a subliminal reality that carries with it a mystical quality.

If the mystics observe the OMER relative to the First year of the First President, then the year 2034 has significance – that year is the one flagged in the 2014 book *"Biblical Prophecy: Are we in the Revelation Era"*, the year when the world experiences World War Three, the war between the Muslims and Christians we know from both the New Testament and the Koran.

But, of course, only members of the Republican Evangelical base would believe in anything resembling a literal interpretation of the New Testament; the same could be said to apply to their Muslim terrorist counterparts. If the cycles were real, prophecy has been fulfilled. But, consider it all coincidental and enjoy.

The day of the fires was also the day Bill Weld announced he was going to challenge Donald Trump for the 2020 Republican nomination.

William F. Weld is a former Massachusetts governor whose ancestral credentials show he is a POTUS Cousin – which seems to be a subliminal qualification for all who have occupied the Oval Office. If we compare Weld to Trump, we find that Weld is by far the stronger member of the ancestral line and, in theory, would easily defeat Trump. Or, he would be an ideal Cousin replacement for Pence.

For those who were infuriated by the 2016 Electoral College outcome, we should note, Hillary Rodham Clinton was a POTUS wife; Bill Clinton was the bonafide POTUS Cousin.

The reality of the subliminal effect which seems to control the leadership of the nation and the historic leaders of Europe, since Charlemagne the Great, defines the nobility appears solid.

Weld, served as Massachusetts governor from 1991 to 1997, and on 15 April affirmed he would become the first — and possibly only — challenger to President Trump in the GOP primary. In real-world terms, Trump is unlikely to be replaced. The only exception is if the Ultra-Left fantasies prove to have some degree of credible reality associated with it.

Over the eighteen months of campaign period maturation, the Mueller Report could play either a minor or useful role in the process of determining if Donald John Trump serves as a two-term President. But the reality remains, Russia has been trying to influence the American elections since the days of Eisenhower and Kennedy.

Also on 15 April, it was reported that Russian oligarch Oleg Deripaska had announced his intention to invest $200 million in construction of a factory producing flat-rolled aluminum products in Ashland, Kentucky – the home state of Senate Majority Leader Mitch McConnell. Using the Ultra-Left logic, the Russians might be investing so as to gain favor with McConnell or members of the Fifth Congressional District. Since Congressman Hal Rogers was born in 1937, his potential successor is probably the one Deripaska is seeking to influence.

The issue is, does anyone care? Buy the Representatives or Senators and it is noted, then ignored, because they and the media will point to the President. But a Passover gift to this chapter came with the mention of Republican Party campaign consultant Paul Manafort, who joined the Trump campaign in March 2016, but had served Republicans Gerald Ford, Ronald Reagan, George H. W. Bush, and Bob Dole – a logical hire for a political neophyte like Trump.

Manafort was convicted of 8 counts of tax and bank fraud, as well as pleading guilty on two counts of conspiracy, but then lied to the investigators, resulting in the voiding of the plea deal.

Based on the Mueller Report, Manafort worked closely with a Konstantin Kilimnik, who the FBI linked to Russian intelligence, and is associated with the previously mentioned Oleg Deripaska. It also appears Manafort was deeply in debt to Deripaska over a "consulting" job. Now, Deripaska seems to be buying his way into Virginia's political machine; which raises an interesting issue, for several decades Virginia had been Red State, but, in 2018, it went Blue.

AG Barr asserted that Trump, personally, was not involved in any act of "*collusion*" or election-related criminality. But, what of Virginia politicians, what role will a next-generation politician take in the effort to undermine the American Government?

Any good businessman or long-term strategic planner will invest in the long-term asset, and that is NOT a President – unless it is the president of the entity you wish to destroy. In that case, the 2020 election offers many possibilities for destruction. So let's look at who cannot win and who has a historic shot in 2020.

Trump tweeted "*I believe it will be Crazy Bernie Sanders vs. Sleepy Joe Biden as the two finalists to run against maybe the best Economy in the history of our Country (and MANY other great things)! I look forward to facing whoever it may be. May God Rest Their Soul!*" [9:24 PM - 16 Apr 2019]

Trump focused on the two best known potential nominees who shared the common trait of being high profile with excellent name recognition, and, therefore, represent the ideal Trump-style media manipulation tools.

So who are the potential Democratic Candidates – as of 29 March 2019? Rather than view them in terms of the January 2017 book, "*Jonathon's POTUS Cousins*", we are going back to the period in which Notre Dame was built, and the common ancestor whose daughters are ancestral to every past President, Hugh of Cyfeiliog, 6th Earl of Chester – the 2nd great-grandson of William the Conqueror and, 13th great-grandson of Emperor Charlemagne the Great.

We can look at the 68th Governor of Massachusetts, "Bill" {William Floyd} Weld, who is the Republican challenger to Trump and what, now, would be a *POTUS GRANDCHILD*.

Trump could replace Mike Pence with Weld or step aside to allow Weld the nomination – thus ending the incessant attacks. If Trump is using his normal PT Barnum skills to attack from the sidelines, the Democrats would have a hard time defeating Weld.

This, then, brings us to the Democratic field which, at this writing, has seen a few release their tax returns.

• **Elizabeth Warren**: released a tax return establishing the Senator from Massachusetts and her husband gave $50,000 on $906,000 in income – about 5.5 percent. Both Warren and her husband are direct descendants of Hugh of Cyfeiliog, with a high level of connectivity to his five daughters.

Upon release and her review of the Mueller Report, Warren Tweeted a multi-part pronouncement [4:05 PM - 19 Apr 2019]: *"The Mueller report lays out facts showing that a hostile foreign government attacked our 2016 election to help Donald Trump and Donald Trump welcomed that help. Once elected, Donald Trump obstructed the investigation into that attack. ... That means the House should initiate impeachment proceedings against the President of the United States."*

As with other Warren pronouncements, the ultimate result would be harmful to the National economy. When Nixon faced the credible threat of Impeachment, the Sock Market halted and then began a slow-but-steady 45-percent decline.

In 1998, Republicans claimed Bill Clinton was unfit to lead the country, and in August 1998 he was compelled to testify before a grand jury – producing a 6.4-percent Stock Market crash; by the time he was indicted, the market had realized it was nonsense and was in recovery mode. It peaked with the election of Bush-43; it took thirteen-years for it to reach and surpass that peak.

Trump's administration has seen a market in upward mode – impeachment would, at the very least, generate a Clinton crash; bestowing great joy in the hearts of both Russia and China. Given the Senate would reject the Impeachment, the act is meaningless and, by calling for impeachment, Warren has called for an end to the Baby-Boomer Economy which began its upward journey when the last-born of that generation turned twenty-one, in 1985.

Based on positions Warren has proudly claimed, it is clear, as either POTUS or VP, she would be a National Disaster.

• Robert Francis **"Beto" O'Rourke** donated 0.31 percent of his income, is a *"POTUS GRANDCHILD"* and thus meets that subliminal standard to occupy the Oval Office.

As with Warren, Beto endorsed the *Green New Deal* which places him squarely across the aisle from those who deny Climate Change and the need to support the many new, far more efficient, energy technologies which are already defining the 21st-century.

In terms of age, at 46, Beto is the same age JFK was when he was assassinated and, like Kennedy, he represents a next phase in the evolution of the nation, while the majority of candidates are septuagenarians representing the era that brought Ronald Reagan to power.

Reagan received a lot of mileage when he asserted: "*I want you to know that also I will not make age an issue of this campaign. I am not going to exploit, for political purposes, my opponent's youth and inexperience.*" But, at this stage in history, age might well be a factor worth noting. It is unfortunate that a candidate would not remain viable if he asserted, *"I am not going to exploit, for political purposes, my opponent's age or senility."*

Though there might be a way to utilize Reagan's line: "*I now begin the journey that will lead me into the sunset of my life. I know that for America there will always be a bright dawn ahead.*" And, by so doing, point out that the dawn is upon us and it is a time to pass leadership to those who will be alive to enjoy its eventual fruits – assuming they can establish their qualifications to maintain the economy, rather than destroy it.

Unfortunately, youth does lack experience, and so there is the reality of the economic damage associated with impeachment and the bankrupting of the Baby-Boomer Generation – this is where the link, Representative Alexandria Ocasio-Cortez, comes into play. AOC is the youngest member of Congress, and the most visible; she is a proponent of both impeachment and a Green New Deal, so will utilize the former to destroy that which is needed to save and improve the nation via the latter.

While Beto said he had no doubt the Trump did something that could justify impeachment proceedings, he made it explicitly clear *"I'm not asking Congress to do one thing or the other. ... I think the American people are going to have a chance to decide this at the ballot box in November 2020, and perhaps that's the best way for us to resolve these outstanding questions."*

• Representative **Tulsi Gabbard**, was born in American Samoa, is a solid *"POTUS GRANDCHILD"* with an ancestral link that is far better than Warren. Her Twitter page has this 19 April statement, *"As president, I will end federal subsidies for oil companies that are destroying our air, land & water & invest that money in supporting renewable energy to ensure our energy & food security and build a brighter future for all."*

Going back two years, to April 2017, Gabbard said: *"I am studying more about the impeachment process. I will just say I understand the calls for impeachment, but what I am being cautious about and what I give you food for thought about is that if President Trump is impeached, the problems don't go away, because then you have a Vice President Pence who becomes President Pence."*

Of course, that assumes Trump becomes the first POTUS to be successfully removed, it also shows Gabbard has a degree of rational thought that has escaped the "Dump Trump" crowd – any success yields POTUS Pence and a socioeconomic disaster worse than any could imagine.

Pence would be the first time non-family member occupied the Oval; the Stock Market would have crashed (losing twice the value of the 1929 Great Depression crash), bankrupting many. As of April 2019, China and Russia were moving into Venezuela, and so setting the stage for them to control its oil; if America weakens,

OPEC justify changing from a Petrodollar system to the PetroYuan and so deliver the *coup de gras* that ends the era of "King Dollar"and its status as the international reserve currency.

As rational and qualified as she is, Representative Gabbard cannot escape the birtherism trap faced by Hawaiian born Obama. But, for Gabbard, the problem is real – Samoa is not, or might not be, covered by birthright citizenship; as such, while it is a territory and so would bestow a stronger claim than asserted by natural-born Canadian Citizen Ted Cruz.

Still, as of this writing, everything has her a US National and not a Natural-Born Citizen – so she is ineligible for the Oval.

• **John Wright Hickenlooper Jr.,** 42nd Governor of Colorado, is also a *"POTUS GRANDCHILD"* whose connection is strong and derived from both his parental lines – which makes him an ideal candidate to oppose Trump.

He also has asserted two things that place him comfortably on both sides of the political aisle: 1. *"I am the one candidate that actually has a long record of progressive achievements of actually getting people together and getting stuff done."* and 2. *"I think we need borders and I think we have to have secure borders. I think we need to have an ID system that works."*

Announcing as a candidate for the Oval, **'Hick'** said: *"I'm running for president because we need dreamers in Washington but we also need to get things done. I've proven again and again I can bring people together to produce the progressive change Washington has failed to deliver."*

• Senator **Sherrod Campbell Brown** is another *"POTUS GRANDCHILD"* – in March 2019, he wisely decided not to run; instead, he is devoting himself to being the best Senator he can be.

• Finally, we have Joseph Robinette **"Joe" Biden** who, like his wife Jill, is a Warren level *"POTUS GRANDCHILD"*. Here we have a man past his prime, and, as a former Vice President, he has name recognition and is a likely candidate. Indications are, Trump would enjoy running against him.

The balance of the possible nominees are Non-Cousins and, of those, only failed 2016 nominee Bernie Sanders has the broad recognition. But, while his asserted policy objectives are widely accepted, this is a man who could not capture a 2016 nomination from a POTUS wife, there is no way he would obtain the necessary votes to capture the Oval.

• **Bernie Sanders**: 3.4 percent The Vermont senator and his wife gave $19,000 on $566,000 in income. Sanders told the Post that total did not include proceeds he gave away from his book, but did not claim as deductions on his taxes. We'll have to take him on his word.

• **Jay Inslee**: 4.1 percent; the Washington governor and his wife Trudi gave $8,295 on $203,000 in income. While he is not a *"POTUS GRANDCHILD"* his wife is. But that isn't likely to help him against Trump.

None of the following are viable candidates, and any not on the list have not been shown to have sufficient media following to warrant inclusion at this time.

• Amy **Klobuchar**: 1.9 percent; the Minnesota Senator and her husband gave $6,600 on $338,500 of income.

• Kirsten **Gillibrand**: 1.7 percent; the New York Senator and her husband gave $3,750 on $215,000 of income.

• Kamala Devi **Harris**: 1.4 percent; the California Senator and her husband gave $27,000 on $1.9 million of income.

• Peter Paul Montgomery **Buttigieg**, called "Mayor Pete"

• Cory Anthony **Booker**

With the end of our second 57-week cycle, and the release of the Mueller Report, the media was again in search of reasons to impeach Trump, and we have as reference a comment by AG Barr on 18 April: *"And as the special counsel's report acknowledges, there is substantial evidence to show that the president was frustrated and angered by a sincere belief that the investigation was undermining his presidency, propelled by his political opponents, and fueled by illegal leaks."*

In terms of Russian involvement, it is important that the media become aware of the hard fact of the CIA documenting six decades of skilled intrusion. That they were helping Trump is an assertion that spits in the face of the Mueller evidence of their focus being in the areas won decisively by Hillary Clinton – and the ongoing evidence Russian fabricated *"Steele Dossier,"* paid for by the Clinton Campaign.

Russia may well have taken a lead from observations that lead to the line from Mel Brook's Blazing Saddles: *"You've got to remember that these are just simple farmers. These are people of the land. The common clay of the new West... You know... morons."*

Clinton was the presumptive winner, and, as we saw, she actually did win the popular vote – but in exactly the way that the Founding Fathers foresaw and wanted to preclude by creating the Electoral College to provide the very same Checks-and-Balances represented by the creation of a House and Senate.

Given that the Russians were focused on the social media platforms that are central to communities Clinton won, there are two possibilities: 1. The Russians are grossly incompetent and so the whole Mueller investigation would have been a waste of money – if it had not resulted in indictments and convictions for a multitude of heretofore undiscovered criminal activities. 2. The intent of Russia was to create plausible scenarios which would result in the Impeachment of whoever was elected.

If the Russians are incompetent, then the media is wasting a great deal of time covering up that incompetence. On the other hand, if the goal was to structure an impeachment scenario, we can understand why talk of it began before any nominee had been selected, and understand why the calls to impeach Trump became the scenario immediately upon the Electoral College outcome.

Russia wants impeachment. Impeachment has always been accompanied by a fall in the Stock Market. The Great Depression began with a 25-percent overnight drop; the Clinton impeachment was nonsense embedded in a period when there was an economic support cushion; in 1972-74, Nixon's impeachment was a foregone conclusion, so the downward journey was both gradual and offset by the demographic reality of the first of the Baby-Boomers were twenty-six years old and so had not yet become "invested".

But, as experienced since the start of the Obama Recovery, the combination of Baby-Boomer demographics and a Baby-Bust manifesting as Negative Population Growth has created a unique period in history which impeachment would end. The end of the ear of financial strength also brings down America. Pushing what can only result in POTUS Pence or a far worse government of the type experienced under Bush-43 is exactly what the impeachment promoters wish.

Bush-43 lied about WMDs so that he could utilize the USA military to murder Hussein on behalf of the Saudis; then Bush absolved Bin Laden of any culpability for 9/11 by declaring him irrelevant to the war on terror. Yet, Trump hyperbole is taken to task. The media must learn to ask about the harm caused by a "lie".

As of April 2019, it is more serious to misrepresent the numbers at a political rally than to knowing lie so as to justify the killing of whatever numbers have died based on the lies Bush-43 told regarding Iraqi involvement in the destruction of the World Trade Center by Saudis. The same Saudis who are being given or sold weapons so they can murder Yemenites in what is allegedly a "Civil War", but appears to be a proxy-war between Saudis and Iranians. Of course, it is far more important to complain about Trump exaggerating the attendance at a rally – especially if that focus moves the nation closer to having a POTUS Pence and finally ending the *"POTUS GRANDCHILD"* pattern.